Exit 38

Rock

Climbing

Guide

By Garth Bruce

Disclaimer

The activities described in this book are potentially dangerous and can result in severe injury or death. The information in this book may be inaccurate and you are fully responsible for all personal injury while approaching or climbing the routes described in this book. Weather conditions in the areas described in this book change continually which can result in dangerous climbing conditions. All the potential hazards are too numerous to list here. If you do not have adequate climbing knowledge and experience, hire a qualified professional instructor. You assume full responsibility or liability when using this guide.

Exit 38 Rock Climbing Guide

Cover Photo

Leland Windham on My Sorrow Bleeds With Such Delight (p. 94), 5.11d. Photo by Bryan Burdo. All other photos and quotes by Garth Bruce unless otherwise stated.

Published and Distributed by

Free Solo Pubishing
FreeSoloPublishing@NorthBendRock.com

ISBN: 0-9723708-0-3

For my little girl Ellie.
With her help I am learning what life is.

> The great man is he who does not lose his child's heart.
>
> -Mencius

Table Of Contents

Exit 38 Rock Climbing Guide

Introduction

Over the last few years, the Exit 38 climbing area has become the most popular rock climbing area in western Washington. The most notable reasons for its popularity include proximity to Seattle, well marked trails, hundreds of routes, scenic views, and some of the best climbing rock in the state.

Remember the old saying "a picture is worth a thousand words?" This captures the essence of this guide book, i.e., it's loaded with pictures. Pictures of the parking areas, trails, every route, and even the toilets. By including a lot of pictures I've obviated wordy descriptions and simplified the book making it very user-friendly. By user-friendly I mean you don't drive around searching for the parking area or wander up a hiking trail not really sure where you'll end up. Locating walls with routes you're interested in climbing should be straightforward because you have a picture instead of a thousand words.

Exit 38 consists of three climbing areas: Mt Washington, Deception Crags, and Far Side. The areas are about a ½ mile apart. Because there are a considerable number of climbs at each area and given the hiking time to reach the areas, most climbers will only climb in one area in a given day. In these three areas there are 20 separate climbing walls and over 200 routes. All three areas offer a wide range of routes at all levels of difficulty.

Exit 38 offers some of the best overall rock climbing in the Pacific Northwest, but there is one outstanding characteristic that is unique among climbing areas - consistency of the difficulty ratings for the routes. For example, a 5.10a route in the Mt Washington area will be a 5.10a at the Far Side. You won't be doing the big lead whipper because of hidden sandbags.

The climbing walls are listed in the book from closest to furthest hiking distance from the parking lot. The first wall listed in an area is the first wall you will reach from the parking area. The last wall listed is the furthest from the parking area. Also, there is a list of the routes for each specific area, and at the end of the book there is a complete route listing for all three areas.

Exit 38 isn't the only rock climbing area. There are virtually rock climbing routes at every exit in the Snolqualmie Valley. They include Exit 32 (Little Si), Exit 34 South (Rattle Snake) Exit 34 North (North Fork), and Exit 47 (Denny Creek).

If you're new to the area, then you should read the introduction for each climbing area to familiarize yourself with it. Pick one of the areas that best matches your climbing ability and hiking time requirements. Next, find a computer connected to the internet and surf to http://www.northbendrock.com. It provides the latest information about the climbing areas and also has some very useful panoramic images of the parking areas, trails, and walls which will help visually familiarize you with the areas.

If you've climbed at the areas before, then skip ahead to Appendix B on page 234. It lists the best routes in all three areas, including the new areas developed in the last few years.

Note: This book is NOT designed to be a "How To" Climbing guide. It will not tell you how to climb safely or what equipment you should or shouldn't use. If you're not sure about any of these points, then I suggest you buy the most expensive climbing instructional book you can find, hire a professional, or get your mothers advice. It also is NOT designed to be used as emergency toilet paper nor as fire starter.

If there is no struggle there is no progress.
-Frederick Douglass

Area Summary

Mt Washington

- Best parking area
- 15-65 minute hike from parking lot
- Most four star routes
- Series of walls along the Mt Washington trail
- Best views in the valley
- Less crowded than Deception Crags area
- No multi pitch routes, four traditional (trad i.e. gear) routes
- 20% of the routes can be top roped (more than other areas)
- Best beginner wall (5.6-5.9)-Peannacle; intermediate (5.10a-5.11a)-Amazona; advanced (5.11b-5.13b) Lost Resort
- Lower walls shaded, upper walls sunny

Deception Crags

- Only 30 minutes from Seattle
- 5-15 minute hike from parking lot
- Good selection of beginning routes
- Scenic views of the freeway
- Great trails to all walls
- One multi-pitch route, no traditional (gear) routes
- Best beginner wall (5.6-5.9)-Write-Off; intermediate (5.10a-5.11a)-We Did Rock; advanced(5.11b-5.13b)-Nevermind
- Toilets close to the climbing walls
- Most popular (because of quick and easy access)
- Usually free of snow and climbable in the winter

Far Side Area

- Least crowded
- Good selection of beginner to advanced climbs
- 15-50 minute hike from parking area
- No potties
- No multi-pitch routes, one gear route
- Best beginner wall(5.6-5.9)-Gritscone; intermediate(5.10a-5.11a)-Interstate Park; advanced(5.11b-5.13b)-Overhaul
- Easy access to a nice beach on the Snolqualmie River
- Sunniest routes i.e. great climbing in the spring and fall

If you've never used a brain bucket (helmet) climbing then you may not have figured it out yet but Exit 38 is the actual name of the Exit that you take off of Interstate 90. To reach the Exit 38 climbing area drive east on Interstate 90 37.3 miles (8 miles east of North Bend) and take a right off the Exit 38 exit. The exit is about a 35 minute drive from Seattle or a 5 minute drive from North Bend. For more detail and specific direction from your location, check an online internet map, for example http://www.expedia.com/maps.

Most freeway on and off ramps are in the same general area. No so for Exit 38. The west bound off ramp is at the same place as the on ramp but the east bound on ramp is at 2 miles up the Exit 38 road. In essence, if you drove from Seattle you get back on the freeway at the same place you got off. If you drove from Snolqualmie pass then you need to drive to the end of the Exit 38 road to get back onto the freeway.

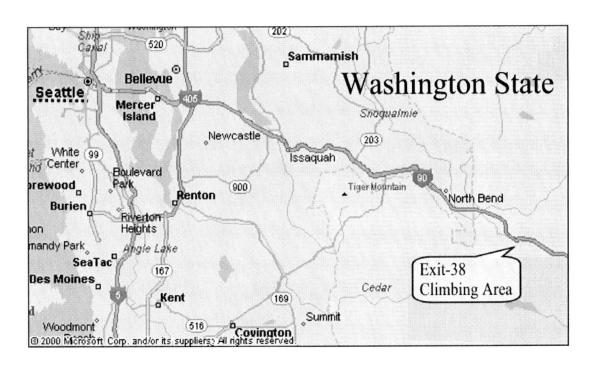

Getting To Exit 38

At the bottom of the Exit 38 off ramp turn right onto the paved road. This paved road parallels the existing I-90 freeway for 2 miles. The Mt Washington parking area is at the beginning of the Exit 38 road (p. 24), Deception is in the middle (p. 115), and Far Side is at the end (p. 175).

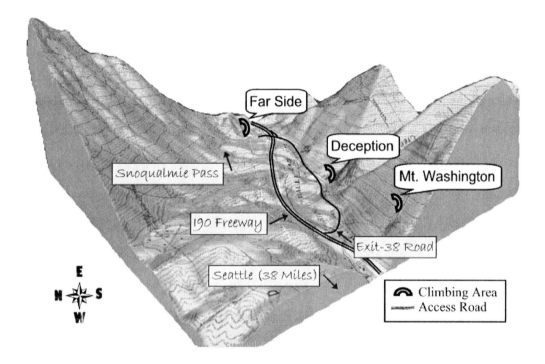

Route Difficulty

This books route diffuculty rating is based on the Yosemite Decimal System (YDS). If you're not familiar with it then you should spend some more money and buy an intro to rock climbing book or enroll in a rock climbing course. In summary YDS is broken into 5 classes ranging from easy off trail hiking to technical rock climbing were a rope is required. Class 5 is divided into several sub categories ranging from 5.0 (easiest) to 5.15 (most difficult).

Exit 38 has routes ranging in difficulty from 5.5 to 5.13. Each of the areas, given the rock type and wall angles, will be predominately easy (5.5-5.8), intermediate (5.9-5.10), or advanced climbing (5.11-5.13). The following chart will help you find a specific climbing area which is best suited to your climbing abilities. For example, if you're an advanced climber, 5.11+, then you're going to find the greatest selection of those routes in the Mt Washington area.

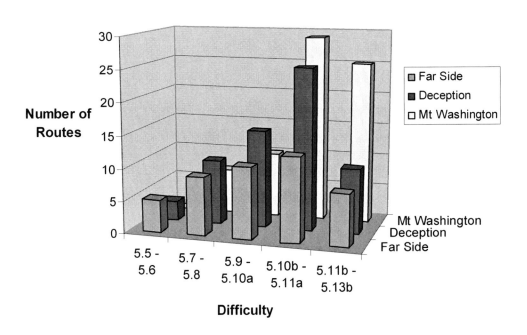

Symbol Definitions

There are three places in the book where you will find strange symbols: on the wall maps (topos), the route description tables, and the route pictures.

Wall Maps

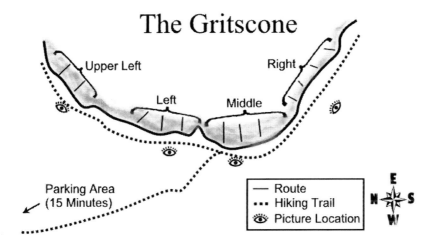

The Gritscone

Upper Left · Right · Left · Middle · Parking Area (15 Minutes)

Route — Hiking Trail ··· Picture Location

Each climbing wall has a simple topo map. The purpose of the map is to outline how the wall is laid out with respect to the hiking trails, routes, and pictures.

In the example above, there are four pictures showing all the routes on Gritscone; Upper Left, Left, Middle, and Right. In each of these sections there are one or more lines (|) which show the approximate location of a route. A dashed line (---) indicates the hiking trail. The picture location icon (👁) is used to orient yourself to where the picture was taken with respect to the wall.

Note: Some of these pictures may seem slightly distorted. Most likely it's just a temporary side effect from your late night activities but if you're not a late night activity type of person then check "About The Books Creation" in Appendix D for an alternate explanation.

Route Description Tables

Difficulty	Route	Bolts	Rating	Top Rope	Route Name	Stats
5.9	C	7	★★★	No	Ellie's Sweet Kiss pg. 211	□ Lead □ Redpoint □ Top Rope □ Flash
5.11b	D	26 (Pro to 9")	★★	✓	Diaper on, Climb on! ! See Beta p. 334	□ Lead □ Redpoint □ Top Rope □ Flash

Difficulty: Yosemite Decimal System number. An "estimate" of the effort needed to reach the top and is usually determined by the person who installed the route.

Route: Letters A-Z. Used to identify the specific route in the picture. Listed in ascending order from left to right.

Bolts: Number from 1-15. Number of bolts on the route, not including anchor. If additional protection (Pro) is required it is listed in parenthesis with the largest piece needed.

Rating: 1 to 4 stars. Route fun factor; 4 stars being the best, 1 star the worst.

> ★★★★   Do whatever it takes to get on the route (bribe someone, wait in line for days, climb it at night …)
> ★★★   A good, rewarding route that will enrich your life.
> ★★   Imagine it's a 4 star route
> ★   Friends don't let friends climb these routes

Top Rope: Check mark (✓) or No. Check mark means you can you safely run a rope through the chains at the top of the route with minimal risk to yourself and other climbers below.

Route Name: The name given by the person who created the route. A bold explamation point (!) at the beginning of the route name means there is potential danger and you should read the beta notes in the route index on the listed page before climbing.

Stats: Ideal place for you to record, honestly, how you climbed the route.

> Top Rope: You climbed the route but wimped out and used a top rope.
> Lead: You started up the route and got to the top without a Top Rope.
> Redpoint: You successfully led the route without your harness catching or supporting your ass.
> Flash: You climbed it the first time without falling or cussing but had some beta.

Route Pictures

There is a picture of every route at Exit 38 in the book. Most of the pictures will show two or more routes. Because of the lens distortion, time of day, condition of the rock, condition of the photographer, etc., the picture may look slightly different from what you see.

Below is a typical picture which has three symbols:

 : Yosemite Decimal System (YDS) route rating number followed by a letter to identify the route.

 : Anchor. Where the route ends (usually two short lengths of chain).

......▶ : Route. The approximate path you will follow to complete the route.

Route Listings

At the end of each climbing area (Mt Washington, Deception, and Far Side) there is a table which lists all the routes in that area sorted by difficulty and star rating. The table also contains the important, and sometimes worthless but entertaining, beta description.

The beta description is a summary of the route, usually written by the person who created the route. It may contain hints or suggestions to help you climb the route but, more often, off-the-wall humor. Some of the route listings will have a explanation point (**!**) which means there is potential danger.

FA: stands for "First Ascent" meaning the first person who successfully redpointed the route, which is usually the one who created it. If two or more people are listed then the rules are as follows:

- Second Person: Did most of the work to create the route (carried all the equipment, cleaned the route, etc) but can't afford a drill.

- Third Person: Did little to no work but bought beer afterward.

- Fourth, Fifth, Sixth…: Friends to whom the creator is indebted for money, bolt and hanger donations, gas, occational rescues, lodging, etc.

Appendix A contains a summary of all the routes at the Mt Washington, Deception, and The Far Side areas.

Here's an example of typical route entries:

Difficulty	Route Name	Rating	Area	Wall	Beta
5.11b	Diaper on, Climb on! p. 334	★★	Chossville	Big Lose Rocks	**!** Wearing a diaper (Depend Undergarment if you're over 18) is recommended if you're leading this route. If you're belaying then body armor or full riot gear is recommended. Also, if you're leading the route clip the hangers carefully as to prevent the bolts from pulling loose. –Garth Bruce FA: Unknown (most likely deceased)
	Possum p. 614	★	Highway Heaven	Road Kill Wall	It's hard to miss this route when you're in a hurry. –Garth Bruce FA: Garth Bruce, Ellie Bruce, Grandma Bruce

Elevation Profile

The Elevation Profile chart attempts to highlight the relative distance you travel with respect to elevation gain. Why? Well, if you're one of those bi-yearly climbers who is packing some extra weight around your waist or arse then this graph is your savior. For example, in the Far Side elevation profile below you'll notice there's no elevation gain the first ¼ mile (hiking down a paved road) and then up a gradual ridge to reach the walls. Visiting Gritscone, which is only a couple hundred feet of elevation gain in 1/3 mile of trail, is your best bet for avoiding cardiac failure.

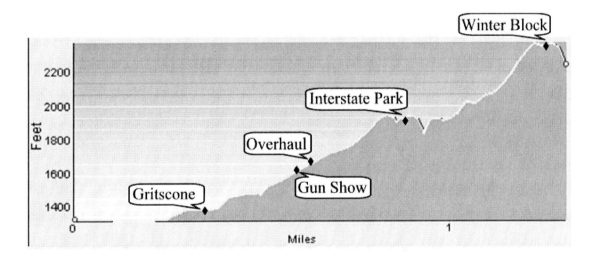

I say? There is no death, only a change of worlds.
-Chief Seattle

Online Reference

This book was designed to be used with the online web site http://www.northbendrock.com. And for only an additional $29.95 per year you to can access it! I'm just kidding about the web site costing money, it's actually free, but it is an important resource for you to use in conjunction with this book.

The web site provides several key features which include updated area and route information, listing of the best routes in the area, climbing pictures, and virtual tours of the area. The updated route information will include things like out-of-order routes, book corrections, and new routes. The virtual tour, in addition to being cool to view, will help to familiarize you with the area so you can spend less time scratching (your head) and more time climbing.

A few of you habitual net surfers might be wondering about the web site http://www.deceptioncrags.com. It has been merged into the new web site http://www.northbendrock.com which now includes Valley View East & West, and the Far Side areas.

http://www.northbendrock.com will also include the Exit 32 climbing area which will be used in conjunction with the Exit 32 Rock Climbing Guide book. It will be published in the spring of 2003. The updated web site will also include a comprehensive route listing table, which you can sort and search, for both areas.

In the future, http://www.northbendrock.com may contain other information. For example, videos, full 360 degree panoramic images, photos you send me, and, if I don't pay my bills real soon, a lot of advertisements. ☺

> *What we play is life.*   -Louis Armstrong

Mt Washington
Area

Mt Washington

The Mt Washington climbing area offers some of the finest sport climbs in the North Bend area. Much of it is more remote and takes longer to access, but is less crowded than the Trestle area and has some grand views of the Snoqualmie valley. The lower crags, especially Amazonia and The Actual Cave, are subject to early season drippage (into June). The upper walls are blanketed with snow in the winter which usually melts off in April or May.

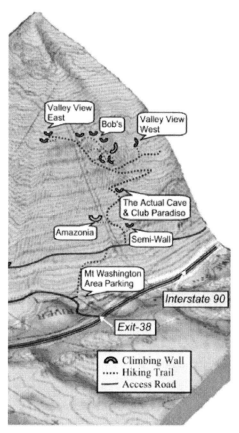

Semi-Wall: As the name implies, this is a small wall with a few short climbs. Sunny weekend? Other walls cramped? Don't like people? Check it out.

Amazonia: Amazonia is the best intermediate (5.10 – 5.11) wall in the Mt. Washington area. The routes are full vertical to slightly overhung, and the rock is delightfully consistent. Local vampires love this wall because the sun never touches it.

Actual Cave: The name is an accurate description. It's an actual cave – for bats and real climbers.

Club Paradiso: Club Paradiso is adjacent to The Actual Cave. It has a couple of good intermediate routes but is often soggy until mid summer.

Bob's: There are seven climbing walls in Bob's area: Chainsaw, Peannacle, Lost Resort, Alpinia, Presto Palace, Slumbersome Ridge and The Stein. Peannacle wall is a great place to start if you've never been to Bob's area. If you think a lot of your climbing ability then Lost Resort is a must-visit.

Valley View East: This area has two small crags with three peachy routes.

Valley View West: At 2950 feet elevation it offers the best views of the valley. It has several deluxe 5.11-5.12 level routes which are guarentted to satisy your climbing addition.

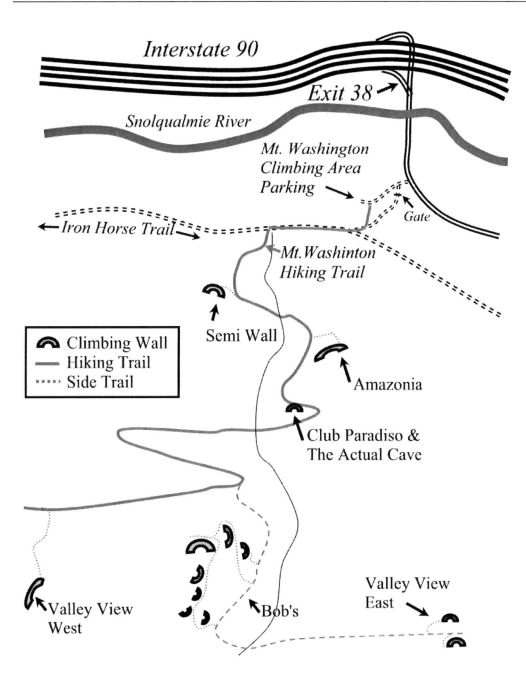

Interstate 90

Exit 38

Snolqualmie River

Mt. Washington
Climbing Area
Parking

Gate

← Iron Horse Trail →

Mt. Washinton
Hiking Trail

Semi Wall

🌈 Climbing Wall
— Hiking Trail
····· Side Trail

Amazonia

Club Paradiso &
The Actual Cave

Valley View
East

Valley View
West

Bob's

Area Summary

Wall Name	Height (Meters)	Number of Routes	Difficulty	Hiking Time (Minutes)
Semi	15	4	5.9 – 5.11d	10
Amazonia	20	15	5.9 – 5.11a	20
The Actual Cave	10	8	5.11c – 5.13a	25
Club Paradiso	15	4	5.8 – 5.10a	25
Chainsaw	15	6	5.8 – 5.12a	50
Peannacle	10	14	5.8 – 5.11d	50
Lost Resort	20	9	5.10c – 5.13a	55
Alpinia	15	4	510b – 5.11d	60
Presto Palace	10	1	5.11a	60
Slumbersome Ridge	15	8	5.6 – 5.11c	60
The Stien	10	1	5.10d	60
Valley View East	15	3	5.10b – 5.12a	60
Valley View West	25	8	5.10a – 5.12c	65

Elevation Profile

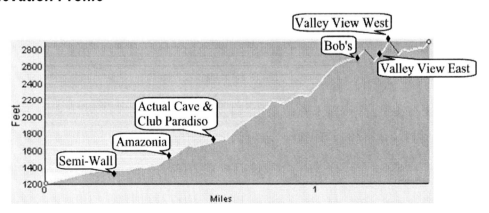

Wall Difficulty

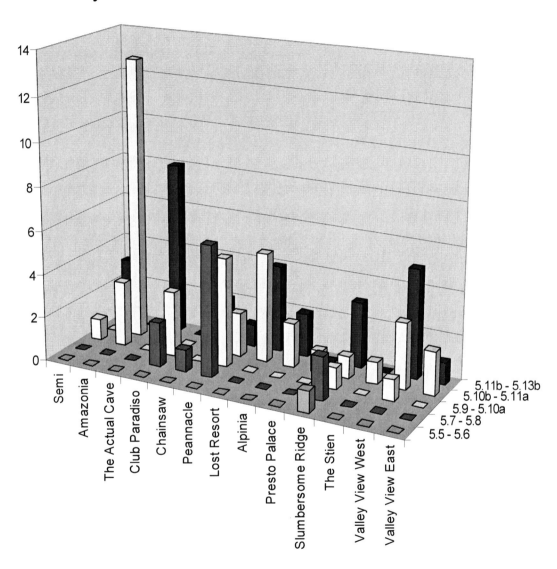

To get to the Mt Washington parking area, simply take the first right a few hundred yards after taking Exit 38 from Interstate I-90 westbound. Follow the dirt road up a gradual hill for 150 meters to the large parking area.

Parking at Mt Washington

The parking area provides access to several state parks and also the climbing walls in the Mt Washington Area. The two state parks are Twin Falls and the Iron Horse (check http://www.parks.wa.gov for more information). Because it is a state park, you do not need one of those ridiculous Washington trails parking permit emblems in your window.

Enjoy this parking area because it's one of the best of any climbing area in the state. It has a lot of space, a new toilet, and an informative bulletin board, but, no latte stand. Note: Vandalism is always a concern at any trail head parking area so take your valuables with you or rig your vehicle to blow up if someone tries to break into it.

Weight Loss Closet

Trail to Mt Washington Climbing Area (and Twin Falls)

Exit-38

To reach the Mt Washington area climbs, take the Twin Falls / Iron Horse trail from the parking area up a short hill to the Iron Horse Trail (more like a road) and veer right. At about ¼ mile (7 minute hike) turn left off the Iron Horse trail onto the Mt Washington trail. There aren't any signs or markers to denote the continued trail but it's easy to find given it's the first side trail on the left from the parking lot off the Iron Horse Trail.

Semi-Wall

Semi-Wall is the first climbing wall you'll come to on the Mt Washington Trail. As the name implies, it's a small wall with a few short routes on a steep side hill. It has the unfortunate honor of being the least climbed wall in the Mt Washington Area. It's not because the routes are bad but because its access trail is superbly camouflaged.

One of the enjoyable things about Semi-Wall is the access or side trail. It's a classic Northwest class IV vegetation scramble. When I first started climbing in the area, I remember thrashing around in search of the side trail. When I did finally stumble across it I spent several minutes getting even with the shrubbery and making sure the side trail would be more obvious. Two weeks later I brought a friend back to do a climb on the wall and I couldn't find the trail. Ya gotta love the Northwest.

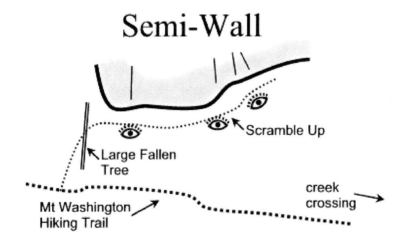

The trick to finding Semi-Wall is locating the following landmarks.

First, find an old, but impressive, log/mud slide. The slide is about a 2 minute hike from the Iron Horse trail turnoff just after the trail switches back to the left.

The side trail turnoff to Semi-Wall is about 50 meters past the log slide on the right. If you pass over a creek you've gone too far.

Notes _____

_____

_____

_____

_____

_____

_____

_____

_____

_____

_____

_____

_____

_____

_____

_____

_____

_____

_____

_____ *Date* _____

Difficulty	Route	Bolts	Rating	Top Rope	Route Name	Stats	
5.11d	A	7	★	No	Semian Consciousness p. 105	☐ Lead ☐ Top Rope	☐ Redpoint ☐ Flash

Notes_____

_____

_____

_____

_____

_____

_____

_____

_____

_____

_____

_____

_____

_____

_____

_____

_____

_____

_____**Date**_____

Difficulty	Route	Bolts	Rating	Top Rope	Route Name	Stats	
5.11c	B	4	★★	No	Semi-Automatic p. 105	□ Lead □ Top Rope	□ Redpoint □ Flash

Notes _____

_____

_____

_____

_____

_____

_____

_____

_____

_____

_____

_____

_____

_____

_____ **Date** _____

Difficulty	Route	Bolts	Rating	Top Rope	Route Name	Stats	
5.11a	C	4	★	No	Semi-Suite p. 104	□ Lead □ Top Rope	□ Redpoint □ Flash
5.9	D	3	★★	No	Semi-Tough p. 100	□ Lead □ Top Rope	□ Redpoint □ Flash

Amazonia

Amazonia is the best intermediate (5.10a - 5.11a) wall in the Mt. Washington Area. The face is 20 meters high, slightly inverted, and has absurdly consistent holds. There are 15 worthy routes on the wall so even if a few climbers beat you to the rock there's always something decent to climb.

The other interesting thing about the wall is that sunlight never touches it since it is North-facing and surrounded by dense forest. It's ideal in the middle of summer when the other walls are heating up. It's actually climbable in the winter because it's low enough in elevation to avoid snow and is slightly overhung, which keeps it mostly dry.

The unique thing about Amazonia is it's built in shower or, as other people with little imagination have told me, a waterfall. The shower is in the middle of the wall and is present year around, albeit a bit more present during the winter. So, don't bother rushing home to clean yourself up after a day of experimenting with gravity. Simply use the built in shower and be ready to hit the town when you get back to the parking lot!

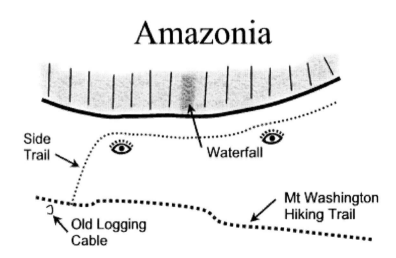

Getting to Amazonia

The Amazonia wall is just to the left off the main Mt Washington trail a light 20 minute hike from the parking area. Look for an old steel logging cable embedded in the Mt Washington trail and immediately to the left is the side trail to Amazonia. Follow the side trail for 70 feet and you'll be standing at the lower left corner of the wall.

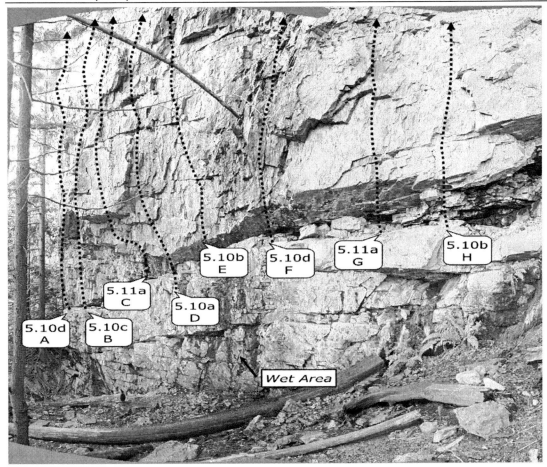

She is so naked and singular.
She is the sum of yourself and your dream.
Climb her like a monument, step after step.
She is solid.   - Anne Sexton

Difficulty	Route	Bolts	Rating	Top Rope	Route Name	Stats	
5.10d	A	9	★★★	No	Arbo-Reality p. 102	□ Lead □ Top Rope	□ Redpoint □ Flash
5.10c	B	7	★★★★	No	Tropicana p. 101	□ Lead □ Top Rope	□ Redpoint □ Flash
5.11a	C	6	★★★★	No	Primus p. 103	□ Lead □ Top Rope	□ Redpoint □ Flash
5.10a	D	7	★★★★	No	Iguanarama p. 100	□ Lead □ Top Rope	□ Redpoint □ Flash
5.10b	E	6	★★★	No	Laceration of the Soul p. 101	□ Lead □ Top Rope	□ Redpoint □ Flash
5.10d	F	6	★★	No	Paste Human p. 103	□ Lead □ Top Rope	□ Redpoint □ Flash
5.11a	G	4	★★	No	Drier Adhesive … p. 103	□ Lead □ Top Rope	□ Redpoint □ Flash
5.10b	H	6	★★★	No	Radioactive Decay p. 101	□ Lead □ Top Rope	□ Redpoint □ Flash

Notes _____

_____

_____

_____

_____ **Date** _____

Difficulty	Route	Bolts	Rating	Top Rope	Route Name	Stats	
5.10b	I	6	★★★★	No	I Remember Drooling p. 100	□ Lead □ Top Rope	□ Redpoint □ Flash
5.10c	J	6	★★★	No	Scrubbing Neon p. 102	□ Lead □ Top Rope	□ Redpoint □ Flash
5.9	K	4	★★★	No	Sodflesh p. 99	□ Lead □ Top Rope	□ Redpoint □ Flash
5.10d	L	4	★★	No	Firewalk On Me p. 103	□ Lead □ Top Rope	□ Redpoint □ Flash
5.10c	M	3	★★	No	Ten-ish Ooze p. 102	□ Lead □ Top Rope	□ Redpoint □ Flash
5.10a	N	3	★★	No	Q.D. Pie p. 100	□ Lead □ Top Rope	□ Redpoint □ Flash
5.10d	O	2	★	No	Enema p. 103	□ Lead □ Top Rope	□ Redpoint □ Flash

Notes _____

_____

_____

_____ *Date* _____

Gravity - it's not just a good idea. It's the law.

Mike wrestling with the
Iganarama – 5.10a (p.34)

Club Paradiso & The Actual Cave

Although Club Paradiso and The Actual Cave are part of the same wall, the climbing couldn't be more different. At the Club you'll find big, reassuring holds on a vertical face. Next door at the Cave you'll find the same type of holds but inverted to 90 degrees past vertical (that means overhanging if you missed geometry in high school ;-).

Club Paradiso is the wettest wall in the area as water indiscriminately drains over it most of the year. August and September are usually the only months it's dry, and even then it doesn't look dry because of the lichen that covers it.

The Actual Cave is… well an actual cave. It's one of the best in the Snoqualmie valley for some real inverted climbing fun. Your climbing skills had better be razor-sharp because the routes start in the mid 5.11's and crank up into 5.13's.

The Actual Cave & Club Paradiso

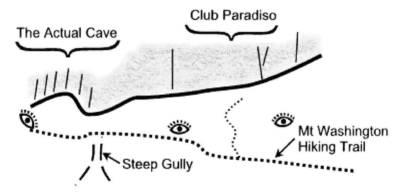

Club Paradiso and The Actual Cave are a 25 minute hike from the parking lot or a 5 minute hike past Amazonia Wall. They're virtually part of the Mt Washington trail so unless you're hiking with a blindfold you can't miss them.

The Cave

5.10a
A

Main Trail

Notes _____

_____

_____

_____

_____

_____

_____

_____

_____

_____

_____

_____

_____

_____

_____

_____

_____

_____

_____ **Date**_____

Difficulty	Route	Bolts	Rating	Top Rope	Route Name	Stats		
5.10a	A	7	★★★	No	Trappline p. 100	□ Lead □ Top Rope	□ Redpoint □ Flash	

Notes_____

_____

_____

_____

_____

_____

_____

_____

_____

_____

_____

_____

_____

_____ **Date** _____

Difficulty	Route	Bolts	Rating	Top Rope	Route Name	Stats	
5.8	B	7	★★★	No	Lush p. 98	□ Lead □ Top Rope	□ Redpoint □ Flash
5.9	C	8	★★★	No	Luscious p. 99	□ Lead □ Top Rope	□ Redpoint □ Flash
5.8	D	7	★★	No	Just Because Your ... p. 99	□ Lead □ Top Rope	□ Redpoint □ Flash

The Actual Cave (Left)

5.11c
A

5.12b
B

Mt Washington
Hiking Trail

Notes _____

_____

_____

_____

_____

_____

_____

_____

_____

_____

_____

_____

_____

_____

_____

_____ **Date** _____

Difficulty	Route	Bolts	Rating	Top Rope	Route Name	Stats	
5.11c	A	4	★★★	No	100% Beef p. 105	☐ Lead ☐ Top Rope	☐ Redpoint ☐ Flash
5.12b	B	4	★★	No	Bikini Girls With Turbo Drills p. 106	☐ Lead ☐ Top Rope	☐ Redpoint ☐ Flash

Difficulty	Route	Bolts	Rating	Top Rope	Route Name	Stats	
5.12d	C	7	★	No	Positive Vibrations p. 106	□ Lead □ Top Rope	□ Redpoint □ Flash
5.13a	D	7	★ ★ ★	No	Acid Rock p. 106	□ Lead □ Top Rope	□ Redpoint □ Flash
5.12d	E	9	★	No	Spartacus p. 106	□ Lead □ Top Rope	□ Redpoint □ Flash
5.12b	F	8	★ ★	No	Cyanide p. 106	□ Lead □ Top Rope	□ Redpoint □ Flash
5.11c	G	5	★ ★ ★ ★	No	Giant p. 104	□ Lead □ Top Rope	□ Redpoint □ Flash
5.12a	H	7	★ ★ ★	No	Mr. Big p. 106	□ Lead □ Top Rope	□ Redpoint □ Flash

Notes _____

_____

_____

_____

_____

_____ *Date* _____

Enjoy yourself, it's later than you think.
-Chinese Proverb

Bob's Area

Simply put, Bob's area offers the best overall sport climbing in the area. It has over 50 high quality beginner to advanced routes and, given it's high on the scenic shoulder of Mt Washington, great views of the valley. This unmatched combination makes it well worth the one hour hike. Oh yeah, a lot of the routes can be top roped, so if you're looking to push your limits, definitely visit Bob.

Bob's area is just under 3000 feet elevation and is usually covered with several inches of snow during the winter. Although the routes are free of ice and could be climbed, most rock junkies get their winter climbing fix at Amazonia.

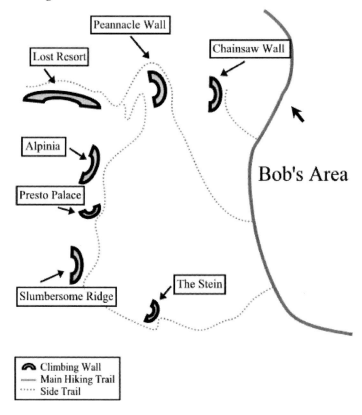

Getting to Bob's Area

Follow the Mt Washington trail for 2 miles from the parking lot (50 minute hike) until you reach a major fork in the trail (see picture below). The left trail leads to Bob's area and Valley View East. The right trail is the continuation of the Mt Washington trail and the Valley View West Wall.

There are three side trails which branch from the main trail to Bob's area: Chainsaw, Peannacle Point Wall, and The Stein.

The Peannacle, Alpinia, Presto, Slumbersome, and The Stein walls are connected by a single trail which makes a loop up and around the ridge. (See map on previous page for a visual)

Chainsaw Wall

Chainsaw Wall is the first of a series of rock shelves on the Northern ridge of Mt Washington. It's a great little wall that has a lot to be proud of. It's quick and easy to locate, has excellent routes, is nicely exposed, and has open views of the valley. It also has one of only three crack routes in the area that requires gear.

One of the pleasing things about Chainsaw is that most the routes can be top roped. To set up a top rope hike to the base of Peannacle wall and then head down hill about 20 meters to the top of the wall.

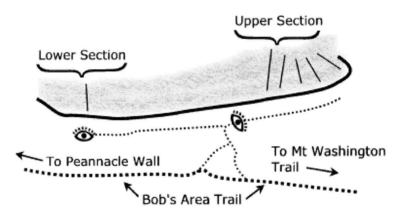

Chainsaw Wall

Upper Section

Lower Section

To Peannacle Wall

To Mt Washington Trail →

Bob's Area Trail

To reach Chainsaw Wall, take the first side trail to the right (about a two minute hike) after leaving the main Mt Washington Trail. The side trail is about 50 meters long and ascends a short side hill to a ledge at the base of the wall.

Trail to Peannacle Wall, Lost Resort Wall...

Trail to Chainsaw Wall

Main Trail

There is no rose without thorns.
-Antonio Pigafetta

5.8
E

5.11c
B

5.10b
D

5.12a
C

5.10c
A

Trail

Difficulty	Route	Bolts	Rating	Top Rope	Route Name	Stats	
5.10c	A	5	★★★★	No	Posthumous Joy and Elation p. 101	□ Lead □ Top Rope	□ Redpoint □ Flash
5.11c	B	5	★★★	✓	My Evil Plan p. 104	□ Lead □ Top Rope	□ Redpoint □ Flash
5.12a	C	5	★★★★	✓	Stihl Fingers p. 106	□ Lead □ Top Rope	□ Redpoint □ Flash
5.10b	D	5	★★★	✓	Texas Chainsaw Cheerleaders p. 101	□ Lead □ Top Rope	□ Redpoint □ Flash
5.8	E	5	★★	✓	Chainsaw Chalupa p. 98	□ Lead □ Top Rope	□ Redpoint □ Flash

Notes _____

_____

_____

_____

_____ **Date**_____

Everything is sweetened by risk.
-Alexander smith

....
Especially your insurance premiums
-Richard Pemco

Notes _____

_____

_____

_____

_____

_____

_____

_____

_____

_____

_____

_____

_____

_____

_____

_____

_____

_____

_____

_____

_____

_____ *Date* _____

Difficulty	Route	Bolts	Rating	Top Rope	Route Name	Stats	
5.7	A	Pro to 1 ½ "	★	No	Crack One With Me p. 98	□ Lead □ Top Rope	□ Redpoint □ Flash

Millisa keeping her focus on
Posthumus Joy and Elation – 5.10c (p.50)

Peannacle Wall

Peannacle wall is the most popular wall in Bob's area. The main reason – a plethora of firm 5.8-5.9 routes on an outstanding wedge of very solid, highly tectured rock which protrudes North into the valley. Without a doubt, it's the best place to visit if you're new to the area or just getting started in the vertical world.

Another reason this wall is so popular is the panoramic views. You can see all the way to Seattle and the Olympic Mountains in the West, to the Cascade Mountains in the North and East. It's a nice place to climb hard and then kick back and enjoy the sun and scenery.

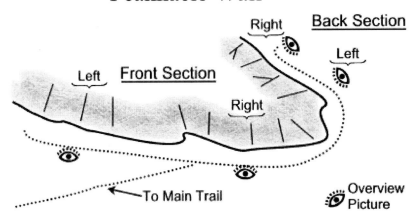

Peannacle Wall

Front Side

Back Side

Trail to Lost Resort, Alpinia, ...

Main Trail

A thing of beauty is a joy forever; its loveliness increases; it will never pass into nothingness.

- John Keats

To reach Peannacle Wall take the third side trail to the right (the first two lead to Chainsaw Wall) 300 yards, or a 3 minute hike, after leaving the main Mt Washington Trail. This side trail will switch back and angle up a short side hill to the front, eastern section of Peannacle.

Trail to Peannacle Wall, Lost Resort...

Trail to The Stein, Slumbersome Ridge...

Main Trail

Notes _____

_____

_____

_____

_____

_____

_____

_____

_____

_____

_____

_____

_____

_____

_____

_____

_____

_____

_____ **Date** _____

Difficulty	Route	Bolts	Rating	Top Rope	Route Name	Stats	
5.10d	A	3	★ ★	No	What Does Bob Want? p. 103	□ Lead □ Top Rope	□ Redpoint □ Flash

Notes _____

Date _____

Difficulty	Route	Bolts	Rating	Top Rope	Route Name	Stats	
5.8	B	8	★★★	✓	A Summer Known as Fall p. 98	□ Lead □ Top Rope	□ Redpoint □ Flash
5.10a	C	6	★★★	✓	Gallivant p. 100	□ Lead □ Top Rope	□ Redpoint □ Flash

Difficulty	Route	Bolts	Rating	Top Rope	Route Name	Stats	
5.8	D	Pro to 2"	★	No	Salutiferous Exaltation... p. 99	□ Lead □ Top Rope	□ Redpoint □ Flash
5.9	E	5	★★★	No	Killer Bob p. 99	□ Lead □ Top Rope	□ Redpoint □ Flash
5.8	F	3	★★	No	The Owl p. 99	□ Lead □ Top Rope	□ Redpoint □ Flash
5.8	G	3	★★★	No	Peanut Brittle p. 98	□ Lead □ Top Rope	□ Redpoint □ Flash

Notes _____

_____ *Date* _____

Connie backs up Ryan as he subdues
Killer Bob – 5.9 (p. 59)

Peannacle Wall (Back Left)

Difficulty	Route	Bolts	Rating	Top Rope	Route Name	Stats	
5.9	H	3	★★★	No	Never Was A Cowgirl p. 99	□ Lead □ Top Rope	□ Redpoint □ Flash
5.8	I	5	★★★★	No	A Castle So Crystal Clear p. 98	□ Lead □ Top Rope	□ Redpoint □ Flash
5.9	J	7	★★★	No	Awannaduya p. 100	□ Lead □ Top Rope	□ Redpoint □ Flash

Notes _____

_____ *Date* _____

Notes: _____

_____

_____

_____

_____

_____

_____

_____

_____

_____

_____

_____

_____

_____

_____

_____

_____

_____

Date: _____

Difficulty	Route	Bolts	Rating	Top Rope	Route Name	Stats	
5.9	J	7	★★★	No	Awannaduya p. 100	□ Lead □ Redpoint □ Top Rope □ Flash	
5.10b	K	1 Pro to 3"	★★★	No	One Chance Out Between Two Worlds p. 101	□ Lead □ Redpoint □ Top Rope □ Flash	

Notes:_____

_____

_____

_____

_____

_____

_____

_____

_____

_____

_____

_____

_____

Date:_____

Difficulty	Route	Bolts	Rating	Top Rope	Route Name	Stats	
5.10b	K	1 Pro to 3"	★★★	No	One Chance Out Between Two Worlds p. 101	□ Lead □ Top Rope	□ Redpoint □ Flash
5.11d	L	6	★★	No	The Magician Longs To See p. 105	□ Lead □ Top Rope	□ Redpoint □ Flash
5.8	M	4	★★	No	Through The Darkness Of Future's Past p. 99	□ Lead □ Top Rope	□ Redpoint □ Flash

Lost Resort Wall Mt Washington

Lost Resort Wall is the largest wall in Bob's area. The pitches are full on, sustained climbing on amazingly consistent edges. The only thing this wall lacks is sun. Trees crowd the bottom of the wall and grow to nearly its height, cleverly hiding it. Lost Resort is one of several new and outstanding walls added to Bob's area in recent years. To set up top ropes, follow the hiking trail from the back (west) side of Peannacle and instead of scrambling up to the top of Peannacle, cut straight across the gully by a large log to the top Upper Left section.

Lost Resort Wall is one of my favorite walls in Bob's area. If offers the best, full length intermediate routes in the entire Exit 38 locale. If you think a lot of your climbing ability (mostly 5.11's), this wall is a must visit.

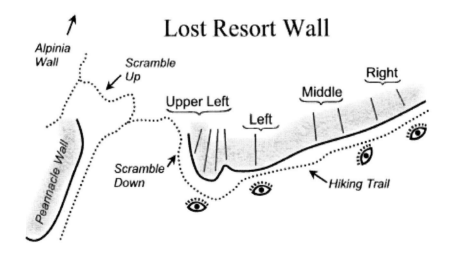

The easiest way to reach the Lost Resort wall is to hike around the back side of Peannacle wall. On the back side of Peannacle (west), the hiking trail continues along the wall for 50 yards and forks left and right at the center of a small gully. The left branch is a short but steep scramble to the top of Peannacle Point and continues up the ridge to Alpinia. The right fork leads directly to the left side of Lost Resort wall and continues down and around its base.

Notes _____

_____

_____

_____

_____

_____

_____

_____

_____

_____

_____

_____

_____

Date _____

Difficulty	Route	Bolts	Rating	Top Rope	Route Name	Stats	
5.11c	A	5	★★★	No	Give Your Shelf To Me p. 105	□ Lead □ Top Rope	□ Redpoint □ Flash
5.10d	B	6	★★★★	No	Andante Favori p. 102	□ Lead □ Top Rope	□ Redpoint □ Flash
5.10d	C	8	★★★★	✓	Appassionata p. 102	□ Lead □ Top Rope	□ Redpoint □ Flash
5.11b	D	9	★★★★	No	Crescendo Of The Sarcophagus Bleeding p. 104	□ Lead □ Top Rope	□ Redpoint □ Flash

Notes _____

_____

_____

_____

_____

_____

_____

_____

_____

_____

_____

_____

_____

_____

_____**Date** _____

Difficulty	Route	Bolts	Rating	Top Rope	Route Name	Stats	
5.11b	D	9	★★★★	No	Crescendo Of The Sarcophagus Bleeding p. 104	□ Lead □ Top Rope	□ Redpoint □ Flash
5.13a	E	10	★★★	No	Crawling From The Wreckage p. 107	□ Lead □ Top Rope	□ Redpoint □ Flash

Notes _____

_____

_____

_____

_____

_____

_____

_____

_____

_____

_____

_____

_____

_____

_____

Date _____

Difficulty	Route	Bolts	Rating	Top Rope	Route Name	Stats	
5.11d	F	6	★★★	No	Liberty Smack p. 105	□ Lead □ Top Rope	□ Redpoint □ Flash
5.10d	G	7	★★★	No	Satoric Inclination p. 102	□ Lead □ Top Rope	□ Redpoint □ Flash

Josh keeps the belay tight as Diane gets emotional on
Appassionata – **5.10d** (p.66)

5.10d
I

5.10c
H

Trail to Peannacle

Notes _____

_____

_____

_____

_____

_____

_____

_____

_____

_____

_____

_____

_____

_____

_____

_____

Date _____

Difficulty	Route	Bolts	Rating	Top Rope	Route Name	Stats	
5.10c	H	8	★★★★	No	Firing Up Bob p. 101	□ Lead □ Top Rope	□ Redpoint □ Flash
5.10d	I	7	★★★	No	POSTINSAN... p. 102	□ Lead □ Top Rope	□ Redpoint □ Flash

Alpinia & Presto Palace

Alpinia wall is Peannacle wall's little brother. It's a smaller shelf of rock on the ridge line above Peannacle. Like its bigger brother it also has grand views of the valley. Most of the routes are mid 5.11 and all are well worth the extra couple minutes hiking time required to reach them.

One of my favorite climbs in Bob's area is on Alpinia. The climb is on the left (east) side of the wall. What makes it interesting is a special rock feature about half way up the route. I call it "Grande Pocket". It has a lot of positive uses. Just when the burning sets in it appears and you push deep, get a firm grip, relax, and then regroup. As you continue up you've got a very enjoyable side pull. It's hard to let go as you continue past but don't let your feet miss out on the fun.

Presto Palace is a small slab of rock about 10 meters high between Alpinia and Slumbersome Ridge. It has one lonely 5.11a route that angles left on a slightly inclined face with meager holds. "Presto Condo" or "Presto Play House" would have been a more appropriate name.

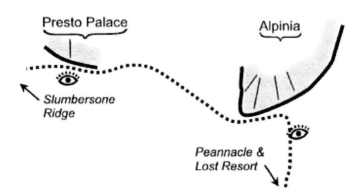

Getting to Alpinia Wall

Alpinia wall is directly above Peannacle wall on the continued ridge line. The easiest way to access it is via the trail around the back side (west) of Peannacle. Follow the trail up a short scramble to the top of Peannacle and veer right up the ridge on a short trail (about 200 yards or 2 minute hike) to Alpinia. The trail continues left around the base of Alpinia and leads to Presto Palace.

Alpinia

Notes _____

_____

_____

_____

_____

_____

_____

_____

_____

_____

_____

_____

_____ **Date** _____

Difficulty	Route	Bolts	Rating	Top Rope	Route Name	Stats	
5.11a	A	4	★★★★	No	Aperture Ecstasy In A Nocturne Divine p. 103	□ Lead □ Top Rope	□ Redpoint □ Flash
5.11d	B	6	★★★	No	Inverted Rain Ascending p. 105	□ Lead □ Top Rope	□ Redpoint □ Flash
5.11b	C	5	★★★	No	Green Buddha p. 104	□ Lead □ Top Rope	□ Redpoint □ Flash
5.10b	D	6	★★	No	El Astronato p. 101	□ Lead □ Top Rope	□ Redpoint □ Flash

Mike looking for spiritual guidance on
Green Buddha – 5.11b (p. 73)

Notes_____

_____

_____

_____

_____

_____

_____

_____

_____

_____

_____

_____

_____

_____

_____

_____

_____

_____

_____

Date_____

Difficulty	Route	Bolts	Rating	Top Rope	Route Name	Stats	
5.11a	A	4	★★	No	Salterello Presto p. 103	□ Lead □ Top Rope	□ Redpoint □ Flash

Slumbersome Ridge & The Stein *Mt Washington*

Slumbersome Ridge is a sweet wall for all levels of climbers. Its unique combination of slightly overhung faces with gentle slab sides offers a full range of climbing difficulty from 5.6 to 5.11a. If you're just getting started in the climbing business, and the easier routes on Peannacle are crowded, saunter up the ridge to Slumbersome - you won't be disappointed.

The Stein is a cute little rock crag just down the ridge with a single route to its name. Much like Presto Palace, it just looks better with hangers on it.

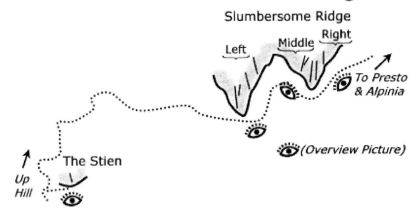

Growing old in inevitable; growing up is optional.
Climb on.

Getting to Slumbersome & Stein

Slumbersome Ridge and The Stein are the last of the upper walls in Bob's area. The quickest way to reach them is to take the side trail to the right just past the Peannacle Wall side trail. The Stein is about 200 yards up the steep ridge trail on your right. Continue up the ridge on the trail for another 100 yards past The Stein and you'll find yourself at the base of Slumbersome Ridge.

Notes_____

_____

_____

_____

_____

_____

_____

_____

_____

_____

_____

_____

_____

_____

_____

_____**Date**_____

Difficulty	Route	Bolts	Rating	Top Rope	Route Name	Stats	
5.11a	A	7	★★	No	To Crest In Violent Slumber p. 103	□ Lead □ Top Rope	□ Redpoint □ Flash
5.6	C	8	★★★★	No	Slumbersome Ridge p. 98	□ Lead □ Top Rope	□ Redpoint □ Flash
5.7	D	4	★★★	No	Autumnal Equinox p. 98	□ Lead □ Top Rope	□ Redpoint □ Flash

Notes _____

_____

_____

_____

_____

_____

_____

_____

_____

_____

_____

_____

_____

_____

_____

_____

_____ Date _____

Difficulty	Route	Bolts	Rating	Top Rope	Route Name	Stats	
5.11b	A	8	★★★	No	Stemming Out Beyond The Grey p. 104	□ Lead □ Top Rope	□ Redpoint □ Flash
5.11c	B	8	★★★★	No	The Validity Of Foreverness Twisted … p. 105	□ Lead □ Top Rope	□ Redpoint □ Flash
5.11c	C	4	★★	No	Imbibing Knowledge From A Mortal Furnace p. 104	□ Lead □ Top Rope	□ Redpoint □ Flash

Mt Wash

Notes _____

_____

_____

_____

_____

_____

_____

_____

_____

_____

_____

_____

_____

_____

_____

_____**Date** _____

Difficulty	Route	Bolts	Rating	Top Rope	Route Name	Stats	
5.8	A	3 (Pro to 2")	★★★	✓	Ultra-Mega Crack p. 98	□ Lead □ Top Rope	□ Redpoint □ Flash
5.9	B	8	★★★	✓	Ultra-Mega Slab p. 100	□ Lead □ Top Rope	□ Redpoint □ Flash

5.10d
A

Slumbersome
Ridge

Date _____

Difficulty	Route	Bolts	Rating	Top Rope	Route Name	Stats	
5.10d	A	6	★★★	✓	You'll Only Get Spanked If It's Wet p. 102	□ Lead □ Redpoint □ Top Rope □ Flash	

The Moment of Morning
(photo by Bryan Burdo)

Valley View East

Valley View East is a couple of crags an easy five minute hike past Bob's area. There are two routes on the lower crag and one on the upper. Much like Peannacle Point, the crags are on a ridge shelf that offers sweet views of the Snoqualmie valley.

Valley View East was the last crag to be bolted in the area. As of this publication it has only had a few ascents but that is going to change because two of the three routes are fantastic face climbs destined to become favorites.

Valley View East

Upper Crag

Lower Crag

Up Hill

To Bob's Area →

Getting to Valley View East

To reach Valley View East, continue on the Bob's area trail past the Peannacle Point and The Stein side trails ¼ mile (about 5 minute hiking time) on a well-defined trail.

The trail leads to the middle of the upper and lower crag. The left fork leads down a short hill to the base of the lower crag. The right trail fork leads up a short hill to the base of the upper crag.

Date _____

Difficulty	Route	Bolts	Rating	Top Rope	Route Name	Stats	
5.12a	A	7	★★★★	✓	Passage p. 106	☐ Lead ☐ Top Rope	☐ Redpoint ☐ Flash

5.10b
B

Upper Crag

Passage Route

Date _____

Difficulty	Route	Bolts	Rating	Top Rope	Route Name	Stats	
5.10b	B	3	★ ★	No	Above the Mantle p. 101	☐ Lead ☐ Top Rope	☐ Redpoint ☐ Flash

5.11a
A

Trail →

Date

Difficulty	Route	Bolts	Rating	Top Rope	Route Name	Stats	
5.11a	A	4	★★★	No	Patience on the Edge of Beauty p. 104	□ Lead □ Top Rope	□ Redpoint □ Flash

Leland searching for
Patience On The Edge of Beauty – 5.11a (p. 88)

Valley View West

Valley View West is one of the recent additions to the area and is destined to become one of the most popular. It's loaded with superbly crafted intermediate to advanced climbs and, at over 3000 feet elevation, it has the best views of any wall in the valley. On a clear day you can inspect Bellevue, Seattle, and even the Olympic Mountains.

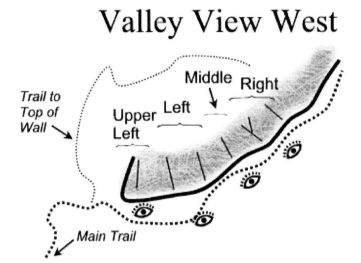

To get to Valley View West continue past the side trail to Bob's area ¼ mile (6 minute hike) and look for a large, old uprooted tree stump on your left.

Continue past the old stump another 10 meters and you'll see a side trail on your left which goes up a short embankment. The side trail ascends the ridge about 200 meters to the base of the Valley View West Wall.

Notes _____

Date _____

Difficulty	Route	Bolts	Rating	Top Rope	Route Name	Stats	
5.10a	A	5	★★★★	No	Stairway to Heavin' p. 100	☐ Lead ☐ Top Rope	☐ Redpoint ☐ Flash

Notes _____

_____

_____

_____

_____

_____

_____

_____

_____

_____

_____

_____

_____

_____

_____

_____

Date _____

Difficulty	Route	Bolts	Rating	Top Rope	Route Name	Stats	
5.11d	B	8	★★★★	No	My Sorrow Bleeds With Such Delight p. 105	□ Lead □ Top Rope	□ Redpoint □ Flash
5.11c	C	1 & Pro to 2 ½ "	★★★★	✓	AtaxiCrack ! See Beta pg. 105	□ Lead □ Top Rope	□ Redpoint □ Flash

5.11a
D

Tree Stumps

5.10c
E

Notes_____

_____

_____

_____

_____

_____

_____

_____

_____

_____

_____

_____

_____

_____

_____

_____

Date_____

Difficulty	Route	Bolts	Rating	Top Rope	Route Name	Stats		
5.11a	D	10	★★★	No	Traverse To The Hole p. 103	□ Lead □ Top Rope	□ Redpoint □ Flash	
5.10c	E	9	★★	No	Rock Party Vagabond p. 102	□ Lead □ Top Rope	□ Redpoint □ Flash	

Notes _____

_____

_____

_____

_____

_____

_____

_____

_____

_____

_____

_____

_____

_____

_____

_____ **Date** _____

Difficulty	Route	Bolts	Rating	Top Rope	Route Name	Stats	
5.12c	F	8	★★★	No	And Empty It Remains p. 106	□ Lead □ Top Rope	□ Redpoint □ Flash
5.12a	G	7	★★★★	No	Empty Martyr Breeding Room p. 106	□ Lead □ Top Rope	□ Redpoint □ Flash
5.11a	H	1 (Pro to 1 ½)	★★★	No	Cascadian Crack p. 104	□ Lead □ Top Rope	□ Redpoint □ Flash

Shaun getting ready to pull a hamstring on
Traverse To The Hole – 5.11a (p. 95)

Difficulty	Route Name	Rating	Area	Wall	Beta
5.6	Slumbersome Ridge p. 221	★★★★	Mt Washington	Slumbersome Ridge	A beautiful juggy low angled arête. -Leland Windham FA: Leland Windham 9/98
5.7	Autumnal Equinox p. 38	★★★	Mt Washington	Slumbersome Ridge	The shorter face climb to the right of "Slumbersome Ridge" sharing its anchor. -Leland Windham FA: Leland Windham, Brandon Kern 9/98
	Crack One With Me p. 52	★	Mt Washington	Chainsaw	Great introduction to a little alpine gear climbing. –Leland Windham FA: Leland Windham, Eric Ellis 5/98
5.8	A Castle So Crystal Clear p. 61	★★★★	Mt Washington	Peannacle	Small blocky roof to chicken heads and holes. –Leland Windham FA: Leland Windham 8/97
	A Summer Known As Fall p. 62	★★★	Mt Washington	Peannacle	Great in the summer, better in the Fall. –Leland Windham FA: Leland Windham 9/97
	Lush p. 42	★★★	Mt Washington	Club Paradiso	Above first ledge, go to the higher bolt for jugs or stay low for trickiness. –Bryan Burdo FA: Bryan Burdo
	Ultra-Mega Crack p. 81	★★★	Mt Washington	Slumbersome Ridge	If you happen to be ultra ambitious and brought your gear then don't leave without climbing it – Garth Bruce. FA: Leland Windham 9/98
	Peanut Brittle p. 59	★★★	Mt Washington	Peannacle	Short, crunchy and flavorful. –Bryan Burdo FA: Bryan Burdo
	Chainsaw Chalupa p. 50	★★	Mt Washington	Chainsaw Wall	From the right end of the belay ledge, a tricky maneuver (with a tree helping your butt) reaches the dihedral on the right. –Bryan Burdo FA: Bryan Burdo

Difficulty	Route Name	Rating	Area	Wall	Beta
	The Owl p. 59	★★	Mt Washington	Peannacle	If you give a hoot it's the face climb behind the Peannacle. –Leland Windham FA: Leland Windham, Eric Ellis 10/96
	Just Because You're Paranoid Doesn't Mean They're Not After You p. 42	★★	Mt Washington	Club Paradiso	The name has been shortened and the climb has been lengthened, although if you get nervous you can still bail at the first anchor. –Bryan Burdo FA: Bryan Burdo
	Through The Darkness Of Future's Past p. 63	★★	Mt Washington	Peannacle	The right most route on the backside of the Peannacle. –Leland Windham FA: Leland Windham 9/97
	Salutiferous Exaltation through Fusty Waves of an Autonomous and Exsanguinating Corporeality p. 59	★	Mt Washington	Peannacle	Crack that crosses "Killer Bob" then runout to "The Owl" anchor. The rest of the beta is in the route name. –Leland Windham (See area triva in appendix D for route name translation. –Garth Bruce) FA: Leland Windham, Sam Hoff 6/97
5.9	Luscious p. 42	★★★	Mt Washington	Club Paradiso	At the second ledge, tackle the short pillar via some very "limestoney" features, then change gears on the delicate slab above. . –Bryan Burdo FA: Bryan Burdo
	Killer Bob p. 59	★★★	Mt Washington	Peannacle	The Rhino Gods once more exhibit their generosity. We are not worthy, but we'll climb it anyhow. –Bryan Burdo FA: Leland Windham & Eric Ellis 10/96
	Sodflesh p. 36	★★★	Mt Washington	Amazonia	Under the sod I found a plethora of jugs and a right handed pinch crux. The first bolt is 15 feet up easy 5th class. –Leland Windham FA: Leland Windham 9/95
	Never Was A Cowgirl p. 61	★★★	Mt Washington	Peannacle	This little filly has some nice tricks. –Bryan Burdo FA: Bryan Burdo 08/94

Difficulty	Route Name	Rating	Area	Wall	Beta
	Awannaduya p. 62	★ ★ ★	Mt Washington	Peannacle	Hike west behind the Peannacle to behold the initially steep face where a traverse on jugs leads to some intriguing slab work. –Bryan Burdo FA: Bryan Burdo 07/97
	Ultra-Mega Slab p. 81	★ ★ ★	Mt Washington	Slumbersome Ridge	An ultra-fine route on the ultra-far right side next to ultra-crack on ultra-nice rock. Hike up the left side to setup an ultra-top rope. –Garth Bruce FA: Leland Windham 9/98
	Semi-Tough p. 31	★ ★	Mt Washington	Semi-Wall	The approach to Semi-Wall is tougher than this route. –Garth Bruce FA: Bryan Burdo 07/99
5.10a	Iguanarama p. 34	★ ★ ★ ★	Mt Washington	Amazonia	Every big hold you have ever wanted gets together for a party on this one. A few technical moves, but this is mainly a jug haul. –Bryan Burdo FA: Bryan Burdo
	Stairway to Heavin' p. 93	★ ★ ★ ★	Mt Washington	Valley View West	Classic arête up the left edge of the wall. Belay and climb from the top of the large block. – Leland Windham FA: Steve Martin, Eric Ellis, Leland Windham 06/99
	Trappline p. 41	★ ★ ★	Mt Washington	Club Paradiso	Named for the Gunks-like strata (no, it's not a sandbag!). Don't hit your knees on the holds as you move past! –Bryan Burdo FA: Bryan Burdo
	Gallivant p. 58	★ ★ ★	Mt Washington	Peannacle	Dark slabby face to vertical headwall. . –Bryan Burdo FA: Bryan Burdo 06/97
	Q.D. Pie p. 36	★ ★	Mt Washington	Amazonia	Go right at the crux. –Bryan Burdo FA: Bryan Burdo
5.10b	I Remember Drooling p. 36	★ ★ ★ ★	Mt Washington	Amazonia	Some truly savory features will provide for some fond memories –Bryan Burdo FA: Leland Windham 05/94

Difficulty	Route Name	Rating	Area	Wall	Beta
	Laceration of the Soul p. 34	★★★	Mt Washington	Amazonia	Similar to Paste Human but the crux is more sustained. Expect over spray from the water fall in early season. –Bryan Burdo FA: Leland Windham 09/95
	Texas Chainsaw Cheerleaders p. 50	★★★	Mt Washington	Chainsaw Wall	A tricky starting sequence gains the exposed ramp above. –Bryan Burdo FA: Bryan Burdo ?/94
	One Chance Out Between Two Worlds p. 62	★★★	Mt Washington	Peannacle	Obvious corner crack. Shares anchor with "Awannaduya". –Leland Windham FA: Leland Windham 07/97
	El Astronato p. 73	★★	Mt Washington	Alpinia	Belly flop onto the ramp then step right and climb the face above. -Leland Windham FA: Eric Ellis, Leland Windham 05/98
	Above The Mantle p. 87	★★	Mt Washington	Valley View East	Tricky slab moves above the opening mantle lead to a very easy run out and jugs. –Leland Windham FA: Leland Windham, Dave Wolf 11/01
	Radioactive Decay p. 34	★★★	Mt Washington	Amazonia	Strenuous second clip then awesome jugs and a handlebar. –Leland Windham FA: Dave Gunstone, Ethan Schwart
5.10c	Tropicana p. 34	★★★★	Mt Washington	Amazonia	A series of cruxes connect several big ledges on increasingly festive rock. If you do not heel hook at a certain point you are a boring person. Truly refreshing! –Bryan Burdo FA: Bryan Burdo
	Posthumous Joy and Elation p. 50	★★★★	Mt Washington	Chainsaw	Same start as "My Evil Plan" then up and left to the corner. –Leland Windham FA: Leland Windham 07/97
	Firing Up Bob p. 70	★★★★	Mt Washington	Lost Resort	Shocking hidden jugs and surprising cruxes make for a phenomenal climb. -Leland Windham FA: Eric Ellis, Leland Windham 08/97

101

Difficulty	Route Name	Rating	Area	Wall	Beta
	Scrubbing Neon p. 36	★★★	Mt Washington	Amazonia	Yet another outstanding route on the 5.10 heaven known as Amazonia. –Garth Bruce FA: Ethan Schwart
	Rock Party Vagabond p. 95	★★	Mt Washington	Valley View West	Funky Flakes and crux under cling lead to a meandering rope drag tour for those not equipped with some long draws. –Leland Windham FA: Steve Martin, Leland Windham 07/01
	Ten-ish Ooze p. 36	★★	Mt Washington	Amazonia	Go directly up the undercling/lieback –Bryan Burdo FA: Bryan Burdo
5.10d	Appassionata p. 66	★★★★	Mt Washington	Lost Resort	A mega-slab starting below the block. Great belay on top of the crag with views of the valley. -Leland Windham FA: Leland Windham, Eric Ellis 06/97
	Andante Favori p. 66	★★★★	Mt Washington	Lost Resort	Walking tempo up a beautiful corner slab. -Leland Windham FA: Leland Windham, Eric Ellis 06/97
	POSTINSANGUI FILACHARYMOS TALITY p. 70	★★★	Mt Washington	Lost Resort	An opus too suite for its thyme. The route name says it all! -Leland Windham FA: Leland Windham 08/97
	Satoric Inclination p. 68	★★★	Mt Washington	Lost Resort	Spiritual enlightenment from a slabby start to a steep face. -Leland Windham FA: Steve Martin, Leland Windham 07/97
	Arbo-Reality p. 34	★★★	Mt Washington	Amazonia	Because it is obscured by a large cedar tree, many people overlook this excellent pitch. First anchor stays dry, but usual finish and easiest descent is to head up right to the "Tropicana" anchor. otherwise the tree is much too affectionate on the lower-off. –Bryan Burdo FA: Bryan Burdo
	You'll Only Get Spanked If It's Wet p. 82	★★★	Mt Washington	The Stein	You'll only get spanked it's wet. –Leland Windham FA: Leland Windham 05/99

Difficulty	Route Name	Rating	Area	Wall	Beta
	Paste Human p. 34	★★	Mt Washington	Amazonia	This and the next four or five routes have cruxy starts with a jugulicious reward above. Over spray in early season. –Bryan Burdo FA: Leland Windham 5/94
	Firewalk On Me p. 36	★★	Mt Washington	Amazonia	A hot crux finish. –Leland Windham FA: Leland Windham 5/94
	What Does Bob Want? p. 57	★★	Mt Washington	Peannacle	I don't know, but he seems kind of edgy. –Bryan Burdo FA: Leland Windham & Eric Ellis 10/96
	Enema p. 36	★	Mt Washington	Amazonia	The name says it all. –Garth Bruce FA: Mike Orr
5.11a	Primus p. 34	★★★★	Mt Washington	Amazonia	The hardest climbing may not be where you anticipate it. –Bryan Burdo FA: Dean Studer & Bryan Burdo
	Aperture Ecstasy In A Nocturne Divine p. 73	★★★★	Mt Washington	Alpinia	Reach for the hole, match on the hole, sidepull the hole, undercling the hole, put your foot in the hole, and save something for the top. –Leland Windham FA: Leland Windham, Eric Ellis 07/97
	Traverse To The Hole p. 95	★★★	Mt Washington	Valley View West	Traverse left at the fifth bolt to the hole at the seventh then it's straight up the jug infested headwall. –Leland Windham FA: Leland Windham, Eric Ellis 06/02
	Patience On The Edge Of Beauty p. 88	★★★	Mt Washington	Valley View East	Don't wait to do this knife edge arête. –Leland Windham FA: Leland Windham, Dave Wolf 11/01
	Cascadian Crack p. 96	★★★	Mt Washington	Valley View West	Steep, right slanting thin crack gains an arête with a single bolt. –Leland Windham FA: Leland Windham, Matt Stanley 06/00
	Salterello Presto p. 75	★★	Mt Washington	Presto Palace	Fast and Furious. –Leland Windham FA: Leland Windham 10/97

Difficulty	Route Name	Rating	Area	Wall	Beta
	Drier Adhesive To The Corporeal Abyss p. 34	★★	Mt Washington	Amazonia	The drier version of "Paste Human" –Leland Windham FA: Leland Windham 10/96
	To Crest In Violent Slumber p. 79	★★	Mt Washington	Slumbersome Ridge	Face climb to overhang then pull directly over. -Leland Windham FA: Leland Windham, Brandon Kern 9/98
	Semi-Suite p. 31	★	Mt Washington	Semi-Wall	A semi-contrived route squeezed in just left of Semi-Tough but a very entertaining crux start on jugs. –Leland Windham FA: Leland Windham 06/99
5.11b	Crescendo Of The Sarcophagus Bleeding p. 66	★★★★	Mt Washington	Lost Resort	Steep block corners intensify to the face above. -Leland Windham FA: Leland Windham 06/97
	Green Buddha p. 73	★★★	Mt Washington	Alpinia	The obvious corner. A divine state of release from misdirected desires. -Leland Windham FA: Steve Martin, Leland Windham, Bryan Burdo 07/97
	Imbibing Knowledge From A Mortal Furnace p. 80	★★★	Mt Washington	Slumbersome Ridge	This route is a lot better than the name implies. –Garth Bruce FA: Leland Windham 07/98
	Stemming Out Beyond The Grey p. 80	★★	Mt Washington	Slumbersome Ridge	Crispy, colorful edges lead to the tricky left finish. –Leland Windham FA: Leland Windham 07/98
5.11c	Giant p. 44	★★★★	Mt Washington	The Actual Cave	It's big enough, anyway. A very inefficient way to gain elevation. The first route at Exit 38 – Bryan Burdo FA: Bryan Burdo
	The Validity Of Foreverness Twisted In Dripping Black Streaks p. 80	★★★★	Mt Washington	Slumbersome Ridge	Crispy and colorful edges lead to the steep right finish. –Leland Windham FA: Leland Windham 07/98

Difficulty	Route Name	Rating	Area	Wall	Beta
	Ataxicrack p. 94	★★★★	Mt Washington	Valley View West	A great crack route with very few actual jams. The crux comes early but the climbing stays good to the top. Need 60 meter rope i.e. route is 85 feet long. –Leland Windham FA: Steve Martin, Leland Windham 07/01
	My Evil Plan p. 50	★★★	Mt Washington	Chainsaw Wall	Prime rock, great location. –Bryan Burdo FA: Bryan Burdo
	Give Your Shelf To Me p. 66	★★★	Mt Washington	Lost Resort	First route you come to on Lost Resort. The crux is a reach to a sloping shelf. -Leland Windham FA: Leland Windham 06/97
	100% Beef p. 43	★★★	Mt Washington	The Actual Cave	Fast food for big appetites. –Bryan Burdo FA: Bryan Burdo
	Semi-Automatic p. 30	★★	Mt Washington	Semi-Wall	Stick clip first bolt or stack the matresses. FA: Bryan Burdo, Leland Windham 09/93
5.11d	My Sorrow Bleeds With Such Delight p. 94	★★★	Mt Washington	Valley View West	Sustained Bliss –Leland Windham FA: Leland Windham, Jim Mallory 07/99
	Liberty Smack p. 70	★★★	Mt Washington	Lost Resort	Triple bulges, trees out, hop clip 1st two bolts. If you use the wobbly tree it becomes "Freedom Hider" at 5.11b. -Leland Windham FA: Leland Windham 08/97
	Inverted Rain Ascending p. 73	★★★	Mt Washington	Alpinia	Slick and tricky arête. -Leland Windham FA: Leland Windham, Eric Ellis 05/98
	The Magician Longs To See p. 63	★★	Mt Washington	Peannacle	Pull out your bag of tricks for the opening bulge then check out what's on the arête above the ledge. Shares anchor with "Awannaduya". –Leland Windham FA: Leland Windham 07/97
	Semian Consciousness p. 29	★	Mt Washington	Semi-Wall	An ape-like physiognomy would definitely be an asset here in order to keep your head clear for the crux. Don't skip clips! –Bryan Burdo FA: Bryan Burdo

Difficulty	Route Name	Rating	Area	Wall	Beta
5.12a	Stihl Fingers p. 50	★★★★	Mt Washington	Chainsaw Wall	This seam rips up the headwall to dramatically reach the prow. –Bryan Burdo FA: Bryan Burdo
	Passage p. 86	★★★★	Mt Washington	Valley View East	Awesome texture with classic edges make this a most do. –Leland Windham FA: Leland Windham 06/02
	Empty Martyr Breeding Room p. 96	★★★★	Mt Washington	Valley View West	Step right at the fourth bolt to easier climbing. Deceptively steep. –Leland Windham FA: Leland Windham 09/99
	Mr. Big p. 44	★★★	Mt Washington	The Actual Cave	Continuation of Giant past another bolt to the top of the cave. –Bryan Burdo FA: Bryan Burdo
5.12b	Bikini Girls With Turbo Drills p. 43	★★	Mt Washington	The Actual Cave	Stick clip the initial anchor (2 bolts), then be ready for anything. -Bryan Burdo FA: Bryan Burdo
	Cyanide p. 44	★★	Mt Washington	The Actual Cave	Currently finishes at the first anchor of "Giant" –Bryan Burdo FA: Ed Sewell
5.12c	And Empty It Remains p. 96	★★★	Mt Washington	Valley View West	Traverses left off of "Empty Martyr Breeding Room". Very Sustained. –Leland Windham FA: Leland Windham 07/01
5.12d	Positive Vibrations p. 44	★	Mt Washington	The Actual Cave	A couple of bolts link the start of "Bikini Girls" with the finish of "Acid Rock". Probably stays drier than the other variations. –Bryan Burdo FA: Keith Wentz & Adam Zeldt
	Spartacus p. 44	★	Mt Washington	The Actual Cave	Reachy gymnastics connect a series of features to the finish of "Mr. Big". –Bryan Burdo FA: Mike & Laura Orr
5.13a	Acid Rock p. 44	★★★	Mt Washington	The Actual Cave	The main form of acid encountered here is flexor lactate, as you heave your way out on this diretissima. One ascent, but the grade seems likely to stick . –Bryan Burdo FA: Keith Wentz

Difficulty	Route Name	Rating	Area	Wall	Beta
	Crawling From The Wreckage p. 67	★★★	Mt Washington	Lost Resort	FA: Bryan Burdo 5/98

Deception Crags
Area

Deception Crags

Of the three climbing areas at Exit 38 (Far Side, Deception Crags, and Mt. Washington) Deception Crags is the most popular. The key reason: it was developed for the newer breed of quick gratification, don't have much time, rock climber. Simple to find, straightforward route access, single pitch, and a lot of good beginner routes ensure it will remain popular.

There are six places to climb at Deception: Substation, Write-Off, Nevermind, Deception Wall, We Did Rock, and Hall Rock. Substation, Write-Off, and We Did Rock offer the most beginner routes (5.5 - 5.9), Deception Wall is mostly intermediate (5.10 - 5.11), and Nevermind is generally advanced (5.11 - 5.12).

Deception Crags is part of not one, but two State Parks: Ollalie State Park and Iron Horse State Park. The Ollalie State Park encompasses a portion of the South Fork of the Snoqualmie River. The park provides trails along the river, and the parking for these trails is shared with the parking for the Deception Climbing area. Iron Horse State park is the old Milwaukee Railroad bed. (For more information about either of the parks see http://www.parks.wa.gov)

Over half of the routes at Deception start from narrow bridges or ledges that were built alongside the rock walls for the train tracks when it wasn't feasible to create a tunnel. These narrow trails can quickly get congested with climbers, hikers, and bikers, especially on the weekends, so please keep your belay area tidy and off to the side of the trail.

There are several rules and guidelines which govern the climbing areas in these State Parks. The most important being – no overnight camping or bivouacs, groups of 10 or more must have a permit, and fee based climbing classes must have a commercial permit. For the complete list of rules and guidelines, see Appendix D.

Being a State Park has its advantages. One of the most useful is the availability of numerous Porta-Potties, i.e., Honey Buckets, Restrooms, Toilets, Plastic Crappers, Outhouses, Water Closets, Bathrooms, Meditation Temples. There is one at the western side (by We Did Rock) and eastern side (by Hall Rock). Never has an overly nervous climber had it so good. Note: The Park removes the toilets in the fall and returns them again in the spring. Year round toilets can be found at the Mt Washington trail head and at the water falls just past the Ollalie Park picnic area.

Area Map

Deception Crags

This 3D topo map illustrates the general location of the the Deception parking area and climbing walls with respect to the surrounding mountains and the I-90 freeway. In other words, there are several closely grouped walls in the bottom of the valley just off the freeway.

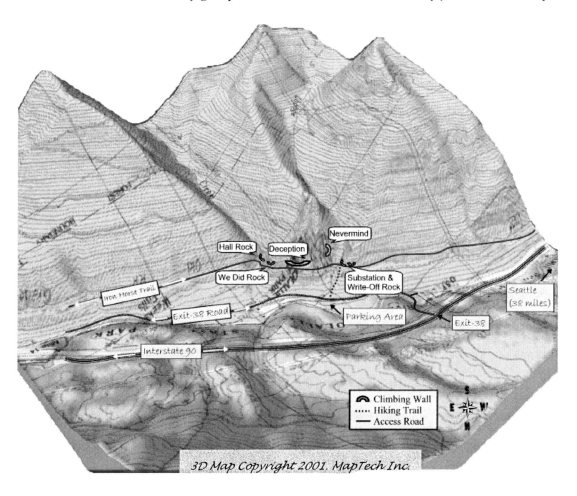

3D Map Copyright 2001. MapTech Inc.

111

This photo was taken from the East bound lane of Interstate 90 freeway. The parking area is in the lower middle of the picture just out of view. The distance from Write-Off Rock on the right side of the picture to We Did Rock on the left side is about 1/8 mile i.e. a 5 minute hike.

Some men see things as they are and say "why?" I dream things that never were and say "Why not?"

-Robert Kennedy

Area Summary

To summarize the summary, there are a lot of diverse single pitch sport routes in a small area just waiting to fullfil your every climbing need.

Wall Name	Height (Meters)	Number of Routes	Difficulty	Hiking Time (Minutes)
Substation	15	18	5.7 - 5.12a	5
Kiosk Rock	5	1	5.11b	5
Write-Off Rock	10	5	5.5 - 5.9	5
Nevermind	20	20	5.9 - 5.12b	10
Deception Wall	75	13	5.7 - 5.13d	10
We Did Rock	15	9	5.6 - 5.10c	15
Hall Rock	10	4	5.8 - 5.10c	15

Elevation Profile

This elevation profile shows you why this area is very popular – it's only a couple hunred feet of elevation gain up a gradual creek basin making it the quickest and easiest to access.

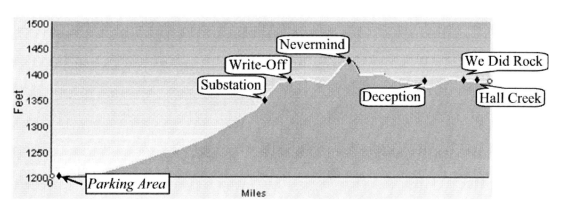

Wall and Route Difficulty

The primary purpose of the following chart is to look cool. The secondary purpose is to show you which walls have the most routes you can climb. For example, if you're just getting started in the rock climbing world then Write-Off Rock has the easiest routes. On the other hand, if you're a 5.10+ climber then Nevermind Wall would be a great place to visit.

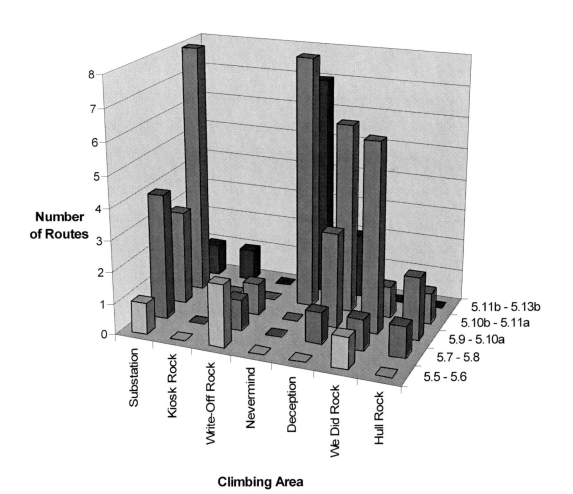

Getting to Deception Crags

You'll find the Deception Crags parking area (in the middle of the map below) on the left side of the paved road .5 miles after taking eastbound Exit 38 from Interstate 90. (See the State map on page 10 for a wider area reference.)

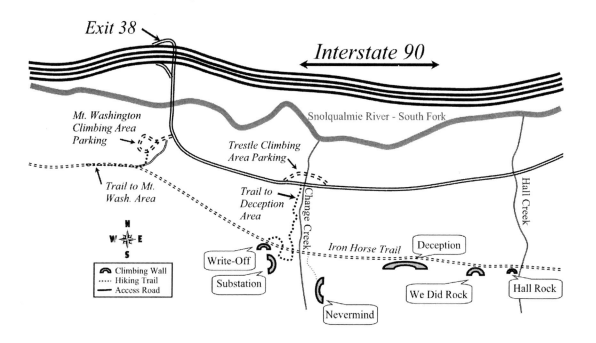

Follow your bliss
                    -Joseph Campbell

... but remember, following them all the way home is considered stalking
                    - Bryan Burdo

The parking area for Deception Crags is actually the west bound lane of the old I-90 freeway. Needless to say you shouldn't have a problem finding a spot to park, unless your climbing vehicle is a double trailer semi-truck.

An interesting thing you may encounter on a summer weekend in this parking area is the National Guard. Yes, the National Guard. At first I thought they were just preventing car break-ins but when I tried to give one of them five dollars to shoot anyone that got close to mine, he made if very clear that they had more important things they were doing.

Substation

Substation is the first crag you reach from the parking area. It has several great climbs for beginners as well as a number of choice intermediate routes. It also has the unique feature of a massive steel train trestle attached to the upper end of it.

During the warm summer months, this is a great wall to loiter on because it stays cool since it's lower on the ridge and shaded by trees. During the spring and fall months, the area between the left and right sections will be wet. In the winter you usually won't find any dry routes.

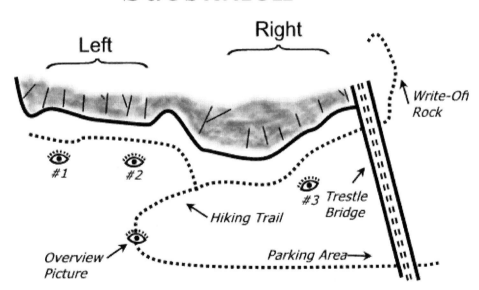

Left Side

Right Side

Wet
Area

Write-Off
Rock

Parking
Area

Veni, Vendi, Evado–
I came. I saw. I climbed.

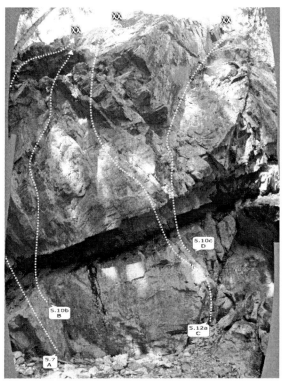

Notes _____

_____

_____

_____

_____

_____

_____

_____

_____

_____

_____ **Date** _____

Difficulty	Route	Bolts	Rating	Top Rope	Name	Stats	
5.7	A	6	★★	No	Turf Safari p. 163	☐ Lead ☐ Top Rope	☐ Redpoint ☐ Flash
5.10b	B	5	★	No	Bwana Be Your Man p. 166	☐ Lead ☐ Top Rope	☐ Redpoint ☐ Flash
5.12a	C	6	★	No	Stick Boy p. 169	☐ Lead ☐ Top Rope	☐ Redpoint ☐ Flash
5.10c	D	7	★★	No	Slippery When Wet p. 166	☐ Lead ☐ Top Rope	☐ Redpoint ☐ Flash

Difficulty	Route	Bolts	Rating	Top Rope	Name	Stats		
5.10c	D	7	★ ★	No	Slippery When Wet p. 166	□ Lead □ Top Rope	□ Redpoint □ Flash	
5.10b	E	6	★ ★	No	You're Only Nice To Me When You're Wet p. 166	□ Lead □ Top Rope	□ Redpoint □ Flash	
5.10d	F	7	★ ★	No	You're Only Nice To Me When I Tie You Up p. 168	□ Lead □ Top Rope	□ Redpoint □ Flash	
5.10a	G	7	★ ★ ★	No	Lovey-Dovey p. 165	□ Lead □ Top Rope	□ Redpoint □ Flash	
5.10c	H	6	★ ★	No	Namby-Pamby p. 167	□ Lead □ Top Rope	□ Redpoint □ Flash	
5.11a	I	4	★ ★ ★	No	Hangover Helper p. 168	□ Lead □ Top Rope	□ Redpoint □ Flash	

> *A young climber will find holds where there are none. An old climber will just grab the stink'in draw.*
>
> *-Chainsaw Bob*

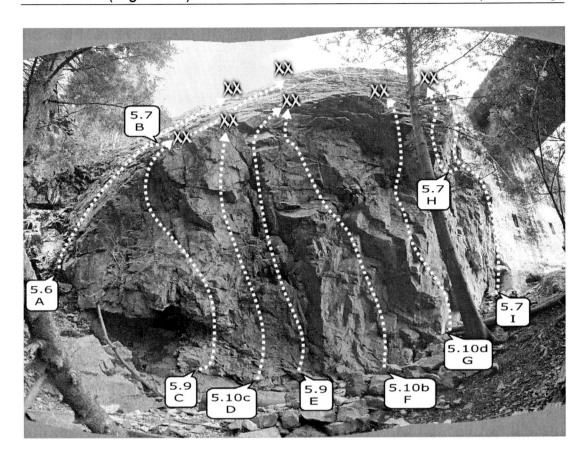

Every man contemplates an angel in his future self.
-Ralph Waldo Emerson

Difficulty	Route	Bolts	Rating	Top Rope	Route Name	Stats	
5.6	A	6	★★★	No	Homo Erectus p. 163	□ Lead □ Top Rope	□ Redpoint □ Flash
5.7	B	6	★★★	No	Rug Monkey p. 163	□ Lead □ Top Rope	□ Redpoint □ Flash
5.9	C	2	★★	No	Primordial Blues p. 164	□ Lead □ Top Rope	□ Redpoint □ Flash
5.10c	D	3	★★	No	Chain Smoken p. 167	□ Lead □ Top Rope	□ Redpoint □ Flash
5.9	E	4	★★★	No	Hurly-Burly p. 164	□ Lead □ Top Rope	□ Redpoint □ Flash
5.10b	F	4	★★	No	Subliminal p. 166	□ Lead □ Top Rope	□ Redpoint □ Flash
5.10d	G	4	★★	No	Subversive p. 167	□ Lead □ Top Rope	□ Redpoint □ Flash
5.7	H	4	★★★	✓	Glom Don p. 164	□ Lead □ Top Rope	□ Redpoint □ Flash
5.7	I	4	★★★	✓	Glob Job p. 164	□ Lead □ Top Rope	□ Redpoint □ Flash

Ellen finding the missing link
Homo Erectus - 5.6 (p. 122)
(photo by Bryan Burdo)

Write-Off Rock

Deception Crags

Write-Off Rock is a great beginner's area. It's a short distance from the parking lot, easy to find, has good novice routes, pleasant views of the valley, and has a comfortable area for family and friends to watch. Needless to say, on warm summer weekends it gets a lot of traffic. To set a top rope on the routes follow the trail up and around the lower left side of Substation to the top of Write-Off Rock.

Take care not to leave your backpack, rope, power bars, or the like on the Iron Horse Trail in front of the Rock. Bikers have a tendency to get irritated when they lose control of their bikes at high speeds after hitting trail obstacles they were not expecting.

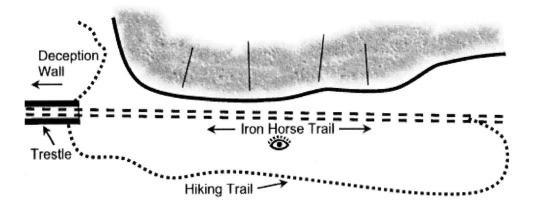

125

Write-Off Rock

Difficulty	Route	Bolts	Rating	Top Rope	Name	Stats	
5.5	A	2	★★	✓	Flammable Pajamas p. 163	☐ Lead ☐ Top Rope	☐ Redpoint ☐ Flash
5.9	B	5	★★	✓	Knife In The Toaster p. 165	☐ Lead ☐ Top Rope	☐ Redpoint ☐ Flash
5.6	C	4	★	No	Mom There's Pink In My Burger p. 163	☐ Lead ☐ Top Rope	☐ Redpoint ☐ Flash
5.7	D	5	★	No	Bottoms Up p. 163	☐ Lead ☐ Top Rope	☐ Redpoint ☐ Flash

Notes: _____

_____ Date: _____

Ellie (age 3) belaying Christopher (age 2) on
Flammable Pajamas – 5.5 (p. 126)

Kiosk Rock

Kiosk Rock is a small and lonely chunk of stone to the right of Write-Off Rock just past the Bulletin Board. It has one route. It has one move. It's had one climber.

Notes: _____

_____

_____

_____

_____

_____

_____

_____

_____

_____

_____

_____

_____

Date: _____

Difficulty	Route	Bolts	Rating	Top Rope	Name	Stats	
5.11b	A	2	★	No	Easy Money p. 168	□ Lead □ Redpoint □ Top Rope □ Flash	

Author belaying? Leland Windham
Easy Money – 5.11b (p. 128)

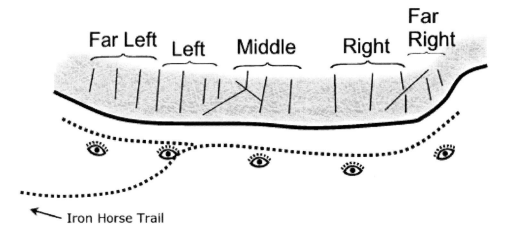

Nevermind

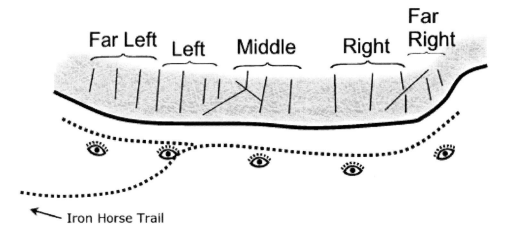

If you're an advanced climber (mostly 5.11 – 5.12) you'll appreciate Nevermind. It has fourteen clean, lean, and mean routes. The routes have great consistency, positive edges, and it's rarely crowded. The wall is slightly overhung and will stay mostly dry and climbable year round.

One of the things I enjoy about this wall is a spectacular old growth tree that starts below the wall and towers above it. It's truly an impressive sight and it's humbling to consider that the valley was once filled with old growth trees.

To reach Nevermind, turn left when you reach the Iron Horse trail from the parking lot. Continue past Write-Off Rock and over the trestle bridge. The side trail starts on your right just after crossing the trestle. The first part of the side trail is up a short rocky scramble with a small hand rope in the middle. It then meanders along the hillside for 300 yards before depositing you at the far left section of the wall.

Nevermind Side Trail

Deception Wall

Write-Off Rock

Nevermind (Far Left)

Notes: _____

_____

_____

_____

_____

_____

_____

_____

_____

_____

_____

_____ **Date:** _____

Difficulty	Route	Bolts	Rating	Top Rope	Route Name	Stats	
5.11d	A	4	★★★	No	Rude Road p. 169	□ Lead □ Top Rope	□ Redpoint □ Flash
5.11a	B	5	★★★	No	Steep Street p. 168	□ Lead □ Top Rope	□ Redpoint □ Flash
5.12a	C	5	★★	No	Under Arrest p. 169	□ Lead □ Top Rope	□ Redpoint □ Flash
5.11b	D	9	★★	No	Negatherion p. 168	□ Lead □ Top Rope	□ Redpoint □ Flash

Difficulty	Route	Bolts	Rating	Top Rope	Route Name	Stats	
5.11b	D	9	★★★	No	Negatherion p. 168	□ Lead □ Top Rope	□ Redpoint □ Flash
5.11d	E	7	★★	No	Corporeal Completion p. 169	□ Lead □ Top Rope	□ Redpoint □ Flash
5.10a	F	7	★★★	No	Neverigine p. 165	□ Lead □ Top Rope	□ Redpoint □ Flash
5.10c	G	4	★★	No	Powerless p. 168	□ Lead □ Top Rope	□ Redpoint □ Flash
5.11c	H	10	★★	No	Hangerville p. 166	□ Lead □ Top Rope	□ Redpoint □ Flash

Notes _____

_____

_____

_____

_____ **Date** _____

For the very substance of the ambitious is merely the shadow of a dream. ·William Shakespeare

Notes: _____

_____

_____

_____

_____

_____

_____

_____

_____

_____

_____

Date: _____

Difficulty	Route	Bolts	Rating	Top Rope	Route Name	Stats	
5.10a	F	7	★★★	No	Neverigine p. 165	□ Lead □ Top Rope	□ Redpoint □ Flash
5.10d	I	9	★★★	No	Constantly Amazed p. 167	□ Lead □ Top Rope	□ Redpoint □ Flash
5.10d	J	8	★★★	No	Easily Amused p. 167	□ Lead □ Top Rope	□ Redpoint □ Flash
5.10c	K	7	★★★	No	Love Bucket p. 166	□ Lead □ Top Rope	□ Redpoint □ Flash

Deb belaying Jerome as he takes a moment to pray on
Neverigine – 5.10a (p. 126)

Difficulty	Route	Bolts	Rating	Top Rope	Route Name	Stats	
5.11b	M	10	★★★	No	Architect Rally p. 168	□ Lead □ Top Rope	□ Redpoint □ Flash
5.11c	N	11	★★	No	Canine Patrol p. 168	□ Lead □ Top Rope	□ Redpoint □ Flash
5.9	O	7	★★	No	Strip Clip p. 165	□ Lead □ Top Rope	□ Redpoint □ Flash
5.10d	P	9	★★★	No	Big Mama p. 167	□ Lead □ Top Rope	□ Redpoint □ Flash
5.10b	Q	8	★	No	Strip Clip Direct p. 166	□ Lead □ Top Rope	□ Redpoint □ Flash

Notes _____

_____

_____

_____

_____ **Date** _____

Your body is precious. It is your vehicle for awakening. Treat it with care.
(Except on the last redpoint of the day)

Nevermind (Far Right)

Notes: _____

_____

_____

_____

_____

_____

_____

_____

_____

_____

_____

_____

_____

_____

_____

_____**Date:** _____

Difficulty	Route	Bolts	Rating	Top Rope	Route Name	Stats	
5.10b	Q	8	★	No	Strip Clip Direct p. 166	□ Lead □ Top Rope	□ Redpoint □ Flash
5.12a	R	9	★★	No	Culture Shock p. 169	□ Lead □ Top Rope	□ Redpoint □ Flash
5.12b	S	4	★★	No	The Goblet p. 169	□ Lead □ Top Rope	□ Redpoint □ Flash

Deception Wall

Deception Wall is the most dominate wall in the Deception Crags area, hence its name. It's about 200 meters wide and 100 meters high but only has a dozen or so routes given the rock type and precarious access. All that size isn't wasted though for it does have one multi-pitch route. In fact, it's the only multi-pitch route in the Deceptin Crags area.

Most of the routes start directly from a long concrete bridge or shoulder on the Iron Horse Trail. This is convenient, but it doesn't leave much room for bikers and hikers to pass by on the trail so keep your belay station extra tidy.

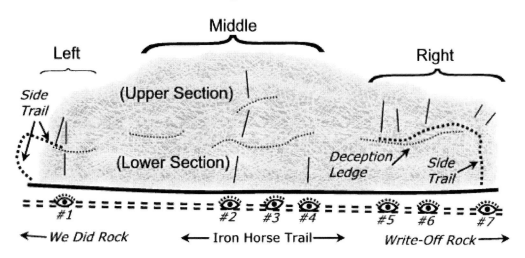

We Did Rock

Nevermind

Notes: _____

_____

_____

_____

_____

_____

_____

_____

_____

_____

_____

_____

_____

_____ **Date:** _____

Difficulty	Route	Bolts	Rating	Top Rope	Route Name	Stats	
5.10c	A	5	★	✓	Side Dish p. 167	□ Lead □ Top Rope	□ Redpoint □ Flash
5.11a	B	6	★★★	No	Late for Dinner p. 168	□ Lead □ Top Rope	□ Redpoint □ Flash
5.10a	C	5	★★★★	No	Just Desert p. 165	□ Lead □ Top Rope	□ Redpoint □ Flash

Notes: _____

_____

_____

_____

_____

_____

_____

_____

_____

_____

_____

_____

_____

_____

_____

_____

_____

_____ **Date:** _____

Difficulty	Route	Bolts	Rating	Top Rope	Route Name	Stats	
5.7	D	4	★	No	Jiffy Pop p. 163	☐ Lead ☐ Top Rope	☐ Redpoint ☐ Flash

AJ Ritter watching the pretty girls go by on
Jiffy Pop – 5.7 (p.144)

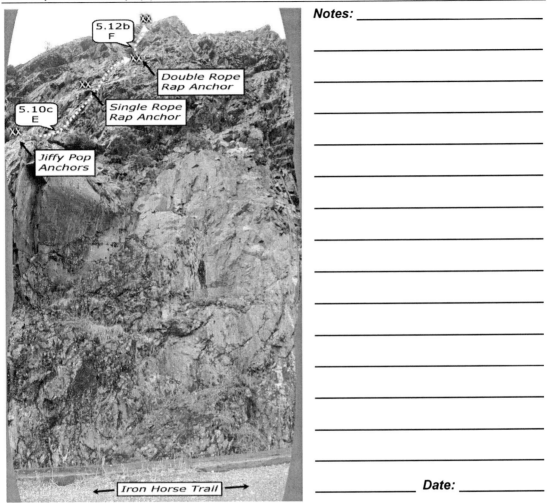

Notes: _____

_____

_____

_____

_____

_____

_____

_____

_____

_____

_____

_____

_____

_____

_____

_____

_____ **Date:** _____

Difficulty	Route	Bolts	Rating	Top Rope	Route Name	Stats		
5.10c	E	12	★★	No	Rat Face p. 166	□ Lead □ Top Rope	□ Redpoint □ Flash	
5.12b	F	6	★	No	I Can Fly p. 169	□ Lead □ Top Rope	□ Redpoint □ Flash	

XX

5.9
F

← Iron Horse Trail →

Notes: _____

_____

_____

_____

_____

_____

_____

_____

_____

_____

_____

_____

_____

_____

_____

_____

_____

_____ **Date:** _____

Difficulty	Route	Bolts	Rating	Top Rope	Route Name	Stats	
5.9	G	5	★ ★	No	Underground Economy p. 164	□ Lead □ Top Rope	□ Redpoint □ Flash

Difficulty	Route	Bolts	Rating	Top Rope	Route Name	Stats		
5.11a	H	9	★ ★ ★ ★	No	The Overture p. 168	☐ Lead ☐ Top Rope	☐ Redpoint ☐ Flash	
5.10c	I	5	★ ★ ★	No	The Underture p. 167	☐ Lead ☐ Top Rope	☐ Redpoint ☐ Flash	

Notes: _____

_____ **Date:** _____

Notes: _____

_____

_____

_____

_____

_____

_____

_____

_____

_____

_____

_____

_____

_____

_____

_____

_____

_____

_____

_____ **Date:** _____

Difficulty	Route	Bolts	Rating	Top Rope	Route Name	Stats	
5.10a	J	9	★★★	No	Won't Get Fooled Again p. 165	☐ Lead ☐ Top Rope	☐ Redpoint ☐ Flash

Wes & Danette staying alert on
Won't Get Fooled Again – 5.10a (p. 149)

Date:

Difficulty	Route	Bolts	Rating	Top Rope	Route Name	Stats	
5.13b	K	4	★	No	Deliverance p. 169	□ Lead □ Redpoint □ Top Rope □ Flash	
5.13d	L	5	★	No	(Open Project) p. 169	□ Lead □ Redpoint □ Top Rope □ Flash	

We Did Rock

We Did Rock is a fine piece of slab just past Deception Wall. The wall gathers a lot of beginning climbers because the whole wall is covered with excellent 5.9 routes.

One of the enjoyable things about this rock is the mini roof. Okay, it's more like a big horizontal crack but for little climbers it could be considered a roof. It's fun to watch begining climbers on these routes. They'll reach the roof with confidence, stare at it for a moment, slide one hand up and over while the other hand tightens on a secure under cling and "oh shit, what do I do now" occurs. What usually happens next is their bad-mannered climbing friends start looking for the camera.

We Did Rock

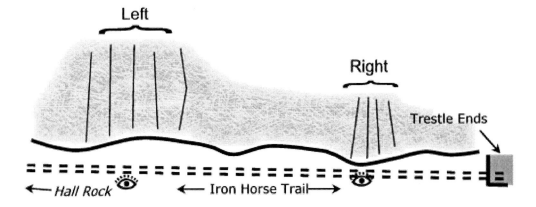

We Did Rock is the next series of rock faces just past Deception Wall to the East. It consists of a left and a right section. The right section begins just after crossing the concrete bridge from Deception Wall. The right section is 200 feet further down the Iron Horse trail.

We Did Rock
(Left)

We Did Rock
(Right)

Iron Horse
Trail

Difficulty	Route	Bolts	Rating	Top Rope	Route Name	Stats	
5.10c	A	4	★	No	The Joke p. 167	□ Lead □ Top Rope	□ Redpoint □ Flash
5.10a	B	4	★	No	My X Wife (short and easy) p. 166	□ Lead □ Top Rope	□ Redpoint □ Flash
5.7	C	3	★	No	Your Sister p. 163	□ Lead □ Top Rope	□ Redpoint □ Flash
5.6	D	3	★ ★	No	Easy Street p. 163	□ Lead □ Top Rope	□ Redpoint □ Flash

Notes: _____ *Date:* _____

Everyone doing Everything on
We Did Rock - 5.9 (p. 156)

Difficulty	Route	Bolts	Rating	Top Rope	Route Name	Stats	
5.9	A	6	★★	No	Black Caboose p. 165	□ Lead □ Top Rope	□ Redpoint □ Flash
5.9	B	6	★	No	Sobriety p. 165	□ Lead □ Top Rope	□ Redpoint □ Flash
5.9	C	6	★★★★	No	Absolutely Nothing p. 164	□ Lead □ Top Rope	□ Redpoint □ Flash
5.9	D	6	★★★	No	Some Drugs p. 164	□ Lead □ Top Rope	□ Redpoint □ Flash
5.9	E	6	★★★	No	Blockhead p. 164	□ Lead □ Top Rope	□ Redpoint □ Flash

Notes: _____

_____

_____

_____

_____ **Date:** _____

> *What lies behind us and what lies before us are tiny maters compared to what lies within us.*
> *-Ralph Waldo Emerson*

Hall Creek Rock

Hall Creek Rock is a creatively named rock next to the trestle over Hall Creek. The routes are a recent addition to the area and the last of the Deception Crags climbs on the eastern side of the area. If We Did Rock is in demand you can mosey down the trail and check out Hall Creek.

The few routes on this rock aren't anything you'll be bragging to your friends about, but the rock is known for a couple of interesting reasons. It's the only known location in the entire Exit 38 climbing area to be credited with a reported climbing accident. The accident was on Erectile Dysfuntion. The overly excited climber clipped the first two bolts, tried to clip the third, slipped, and grounded. Ouch. The second reason it's known is that it has the shortest sport route in the North Bend area, aptly named "Sport Sickness". It's about 5 meters high with two generous bolts.

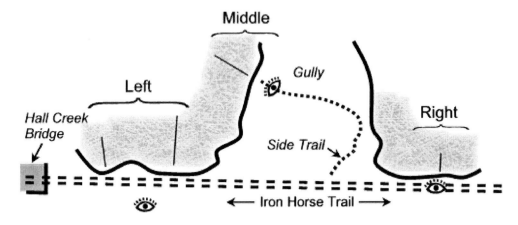

Getting to Hall Creek Rock

To reach Hall Creek Rock, continue 50 meters past We Did Rock. It's a couple of short rock outcrops on the right side. If you cross over the Hall Creek trestle, turn slowly around, act like you were looking at the scenery, and walk back to the start of the bridge and look up and left.

Hall Creek Rock (Left)

Hall Creek Trestle

Iron Horse Trail

Difficulty	Route	Bolts	Rating	Top Rope	Route Name	Stats	
5.8	A	3	★	No	Erectile Dysfunction ! See Beta p. 165	□ Lead □ Top Rope	□ Redpoint □ Flash
5.8	B	6	★★	No	Occam's Razor p. 164	□ Lead □ Top Rope	□ Redpoint □ Flash

Notes: _____

_____

_____   *Date:* _____

Notes: _____

_____

_____

_____

_____

_____

_____

_____

_____

_____

_____

_____

_____

_____

_____

_____

_____

_____

_____

_____ **Date:** _____

Difficulty	Route	Bolts	Rating	Top Rope	Route Name	Stats	
5.10a	C	6	★ ★	No	Rhino Rave p. 165	□ Lead □ Top Rope	□ Redpoint □ Flash

Difficulty	Route	Bolts	Rating	Top Rope	Route Name	Stats	
5.10c	D	2	★	No	Sport Sickness p. 167	□ Lead □ Top Rope	□ Redpoint □ Flash

Deception Crags Route Listings

Difficulty	Route Name	Rating	Area	Wall	Beta
5.5	Flammable Pajamas p. 126	★ ★	Deception	Write-Off Rock	A good beginner slab route – best if not done in flaming pajamas. –Garth Bruce FA: Bryan Burdo
5.6	Homo Erectus p. 122	★ ★ ★	Deception	Substation	Wonderfully textured slab meandering. –Bryan Burdo FA: Bryan Burdo
	Mom There's Pink In My Burger p. 126	★ ★	Deception	Write-Off Rock	A fun route that makes a great first lead. –Bryan Burdo FA: Bryan Burdo
	Easy Street p. 154	★ ★	Deception	We Did Rock	It's good to be on easy street. –Garth Bruce FA: Curtis "Lucky" Gibson 9/02
5.7	Rug Monkey p. 122	★ ★ ★	Deception	Substation	Ironically, one of the easiest routes in the area has perhaps the fewest holds. –Bryan Burdo FA: Bryan Burdo
	Bottoms Up p. 126	★ ★	Deception	Write-Off Rock	Don't forget to clip the first hanger or your bottom might bounce. –Garth Bruce FA: Jean Pierre Banville
	Turf Safari p. 119	★	Deception	Substation	Stay as far left as you can without wandering off into the woods. –Bryan Burdo FA: Bryan Burdo
	Jiffy Pop p. 144	★	Deception	Deception	Easy face starts to the left of the prominent "cut-out" prow. –Bryan Burdo FA: Mike Orr
	Your Sister p. 154	★	Deception	We Did Rock	You may find yourself wondering why you did this one. –Garth Bruce FA: Bryan Burdo

...fficulty	Route Name	Rating	Area	Wall	Beta
5.8	Glom Don p. 122	★ ★ ★	Deception	Substation	Lie back directly up the cement/rock interface to the top. Warning: Do not attempt to use protection in this crack - the concrete is very weak. –Bryan Burdo FA: Bryan Burdo
	Glob Job p. 122	★ ★ ★	Deception	Substation	Start at the rock/trestle juncture and exit left to the arête. FA: Bryan Burdo
	Occam's Razor p. 160	★ ★	Deception	Hall Rock	Straight up and over the budge will get you to the anchor. Long runners on it will ease the wear on your rope. –Garth Bruce FA: Jean Pierre Banville
5.9	Absolutely Nothing p. 156	★ ★ ★ ★	Deception	We Did Rock	Excellent slab. –Bryan Burdo FA: Bryan Burdo
	Hurly-Burly p. 122	★ ★ ★	Deception	Substation	Follows the heavily featured fault. –Bryan Burdo FA: Bryan Burdo
	Some Drugs p. 156	★ ★ ★	Deception	We Did Rock	Clever comer at junction of slab and buttress. –Bryan Burdo FA: Bryan Burdo
	Blockhead p. 156	★ ★ ★	Deception	We Did Rock	Steep face just right of slab. –Bryan Burdo FA: Mike Orr
	Underground Economy p. 147	★ ★	Deception	Deception Wall	Starts just off the trail on the concrete bridge footing. If you're belaying a climber who is twice your weight then strapping yourself to the old railroad tie might be a good idea. –Garth Bruce FA: Bryan Burdo
	Primordial Blues p. 120	★ ★	Deception	Substation	Anchors are reached via the start of "Rug Monkey"–Bryan Burdo FA: Bryan Burdo
	Knife In The Toaster p. 126	★ ★	Deception	Write-Off Rock	A comforting slab leads to a jolt at the end. –Bryan Burdo FA: Bryan Burdo

Difficulty	Route Name	Rating	Area	Wall	Beta
	Black Caboose p. 156	★ ★	Deception	We Did Rock	FA: Curtis "Lucky" Gibson, Jim Yoder 8/98
	Strip Clip p. 138	★ ★	Deception	Nevermind	Start as for "Big Mama" then continue up the ramp to finish via the slab above to the anchors of "Culture Shock." Variant start begins directly on tricky face to the right. –Bryan Burdo FA: Mack Johnson
	Erectile Dysfunction p. 160	★	Deception	Hall Creek	! Be careful when clipping the second bolt or an erectile dysfuntion will be the least of your worries i.e. you'll hit the lower ledge. –Garth Bruce FA: Jean Pierre Banville
	Sobriety p. 156	★	Deception	We Did Rock	An awkward sequence of moves will get you up and over the lip to some smooth climbing. –Garth Bruce FA: Brent Kertzman
5.10a	Just Desert p. 143	★ ★ ★ ★	Deception	Deception	There's always room for this delectable corner-type-thing. Can be approached via Side Dish or by hiking down the RR grade about 25 yards and heading through the woods from the left. –Bryan Burdo FA: Bryan Burdo
	Lovey-Dovey p. 120	★ ★ ★	Deception	Substation	"You so good to me, bebby..." Stem the obvious dihedral. –Bryan Burdo FA: Bryan Burdo
	Won't Get Fooled Again p. 149	★ ★ ★	Deception	Deception	A full 80' of climbing with a tricky comer at the top. If bolted, the direct finish is about 5.10b, with reachy jugs. –Bryan Burdo FA: Bryan Burdo
	Neverigine p. 134	★ ★ ★	Deception	Nevermind	Jugs-ramp-face angling up and right. -Bryan Burdo FA: Bryan Burdo
	Rhino Rave p. 161	★ ★	Deception	Hall Rock	Starts off on some fat jugs and finishes on some lean crimpers. –Garth Bruce FA: Curtis "Lucky" Gibson, Mary Hume

Difficulty	Route Name	Rating	Area	Wall	Beta
	My X Wife (short and easy) p. 154	★	Deception	We Did Rock	It's short and easy and all my buds have done her. –Lucky FA: Curtis "Lucky" Gibson 9-18-98
5.10b	You're Only Nice To Me When You're Wet p. 120	★ ★	Deception	Substation	Variation of "You're Only Nice To Me When I Tie You Up". Depart leftward before 3rd bolt to finish via "Slippery When Wet". Long runner for fourth bolt helpful. -Bryan Burdo FA: Bryan Burdo
	Bwana Be Your Man p. 119	★	Deception	Substation	This route shares most of its bolts with its neighbor on the left, but stays right of them for a completely different climb-Bryan Burdo FA: Bryan Burdo
	Subliminal p. 120	★ ★	Deception	Substation	It's more of a route than it appears. -Bryan Burdo FA: Bryan Burdo
	Strip Clip (Direct) p. 138	★	Deception	Nevermind	"Strip Clip" short cut or "Big Mama" variation. – Garth Bruce FA: Mack Johnson
5.10c	Love Bucket p. 136	★ ★ ★	Deception	Nevermind	Same first bolt as "Easily" then straight up. –Bryan Burdo FA: CP Little
	Slippery When Wet p. 120	★ ★	Deception	Substation	The opening moves are the (reachy) crux; pulling on the first draw eases the grade a bit and accesses the tricky stuff above. -Bryan Burdo FA: Bryan Burdo
	Powerless p. 134	★ ★	Deception	Nevermind	Start on Neverigine and then take the first exit left and cruise up for a nice ride to the ledge. –Garth Bruce FA: Mack Johnson
	Rat Face p. 144	★ ★	Deception	Deception	From the top of Jiffy Pop continue up and right on a serious of swing moves. Half way to the upper ledge there is a set of chains for a 50 meter rap. If you climb higher you'll need two ropes to rap to the trestle. –Garth Bruce FA: Mike Orr

Difficulty	Route Name	Rating	Area	Wall	Beta
	Chain Smoken p. 122	★ ★	Deception	Substation	Your forearms will be smoken when you reach the chains. –Garth Bruce FA: Dale Fleshman, Curtis "Lucky" Gibson 9/01
	Namby-Pamby p. 120	★ ★	Deception	Substation	Gymnastic finish on an exposed arete. -Bryan Burdo FA: Bryan Burdo
	Side Dish p. 143	★	Deception	Deception	Originally given 5.10a but key holds departed. –Bryan Burdo FA: Bryan Burdo
	The Joke p. 154	★	Deception	We Did Rock	Deceptively hard bolder problem. –Duncan Smith FA: Mike Orr
	Sport Sickness p. 161	★	Deception	Hall Rock	It's good to be tall! –Garth Bruce FA: Curtis "Lucky" Gibson, Jim Bonner 7/01
5.10d	Big Mama p. 138	★ ★ ★	Deception	Nevermind	Everybody seems to love her. –Bryan Burdo FA: CP Little
	Constantly Amazed p. 136	★ ★ ★	Deception	Nevermind	Starting hangers are painted black so you know which, of the three possible hangers, to clip. Continue past the chain to the dramatic conclusion via a chain and "Rhinohorn." -Bryan Burdo FA: Bryan Burdo
	Easily Amused p. 136	★ ★ ★	Deception	Nevermind	Follow dark-colored hangers up and left (bouldery start), crossing Neverigine and finishing at the same anchors. Going all the way to the top is a buttload of 5. 10. -Bryan Burdo FA: Bryan Burdo
	The Underture p. 149	★ ★ ★	Deception	Substation	This section of the wall features a rarity on Rhino - sustained pure vertical climbing. Can be taken to "Happy" anchor. –Bryan Burdo FA: Bryan Burdo
	Subversive p. 122	★ ★	Deception	Substation	It helps to be sneaky to deal with this overhanging slab climbing stuff. -Bryan Burdo FA: Bryan Burdo

Difficulty	Route Name	Rating	Area	Wall	Beta
	You're Only Nice To Me When I Tie You Up p. 120	★★	Deception	Substation	Taking the final crux on the left is easier but more devious, climbing it directly on the right is more strenuous. -Bryan Burdo FA: Bryan Burdo
5.11a	Hangover Helper p. 120	★★★	Deception	Substation	You'll pay if you don't save a little for the end of this route. –Garth Bruce FA: Bryan Burdo
	Late For Dinner p. 143	★★★	Deception	Deception	Climbing this route is like eating at a fancy restaurant – there's not a lot on the plate but what's there is excellent. –Garth Bruce FA: Curtis "Lucky" Gibson, Dale Fleshman, Tucker Carlton 10/99
	Steep Street p. 133	★★★	Deception	Nevermind	Classic burliness. –Bryan Burdo FA: CP Little
	The Overture p. 148	★★★★	Deception	Deception	Quick tempo start and a rousing grand finale. –Garth Bruce FA: Bryan Burdo
	Architect Rally p. 138	★★★	Deception	Nevermind	Nicely sustained, with lots of clipping practice. –Bryan Burdo FA: CP Little
5.11b	Negatherion p. 134	★★★	Deception	Nevermind	Classic verticality. –Bryan Burdo FA: Leland Windham 6/94
	Easy Money p. 128	★	Deception	Kiosk	The best thing about this route is you can belay from the toilet (although most climbers will be done before the belayer can get their pants down ;-) – Garth Bruce FA: Denis Crowley, Tim Mulligan 9/01
5.11c	Canine Patrol p. 136	★★	Deception	Nevermind	Steep route with a thin crux which causes many to "dog." –Bryan Burdo FA: CP Little
	Hangerville p. 134	★	Deception	Nevermind	FA: Mack Johnson

168

Difficulty	Route Name	Rating	Area	Wall	Beta
5.11d	Rude Road p. 133	★ ★ ★	Deception	Nevermind	FA: Mack Johnson
	Corporeal Completion p. 134	★ ★	Deception	Nevermind	Begins on the black streak, then follows the right-hand bolts off of the ledge. –Leland Windham FA: Leland Windham 7/94
5.12a	Culture Shock p. 140	★ ★	Deception	Nevermind	The two routes on this steep face offer some savory sauce for all of the vertical buffet to the left. –Bryan Burdo FA: John Heiman
	Under Arrest p. 133	★ ★	Deception	Nevermind	Start from the left; the bouldery direct start pushes it toward 12b. –Bryan Burdo FA: CP Little
	Stick Boy p. 119	★	Deception	Substation	The start is the very bouldery crux on frustrating holds. Stick-clipping might make things more enjoyable. –Bryan Burdo FA: Mike Orr
5.12b	The Goblet p. 138	★ ★	Deception	Nevermind	Excellent moves in a compact package. –Bryan Burdo FA: CP Little
	I Can Fly p. 146	★	Deception	Deception	All the fun is getting out of the gate on this route FA: Mike Orr
5.13b	Deliverance p. 151	★	Deception	Deception	Short and savage, with the cruxes being the clips (probably - 5.12+ on TR). This was the first of many 5.13's for local stud-muffin Mike Orr –Bryan Burdo FA: Mike Orr
5.13d	Open Project p. 151	★	Deception	Deception	Reportedly hard 5.13 –Bryan Burdo FA: Mike Orr

Far Side
Area

Far Side

The Far Side climbing area is at the end of the Exit 38 road. It offers a wide range of climbs from overhanging advanced to easier slab routes. Unlike the Deception and Mt Washington area, most of the walls face south and receive more than enough sunshine.

There are five separate climbing areas at Far Side: Overhaul, Gritscone, Gun Show, Interstate Park, and Winter Block. Gritscone and Interstate Park offer the best beginning level climbs (5.5 – 5.8) and Gun Show has the best slab route in the valley.

One of the enjoyable things about this climbing area is that there isn't much climbing in the area. You can usually walk up and grab any route, day or night. So, if you experience a little route constipation in the Deception Crags area, head over to Far Side. The routes are all single pitch sport climbs so don't worry about bringing that big rack or extra rope.

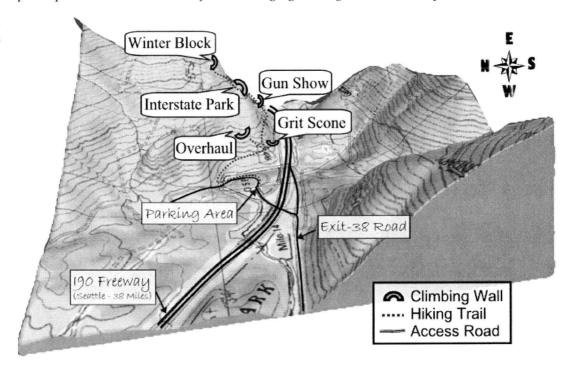

172

Area Summary

Everything you need to know, and a lot you didn't need to know, about the area is nicely formatted in the following table:

Wall Name	Height (Meters)	Number of Routes	Hiking Time (Minutes)	Elevation Gain (Feet)
Gritscone	10	11	10	200
Overhaul	20	29	20	550
Gun Show	35	2	25	612
Interstate Park	10 - 20	18	25	704
Winter Block	15	4	35	1043

Elevation Profile

As shown in the graph below, Gritscone is an easy hike given it's lowest in elevation and closest to the parking area. Winterblock is the highest in elevation and furthest so try to con your climbing partner into carrying the rope.

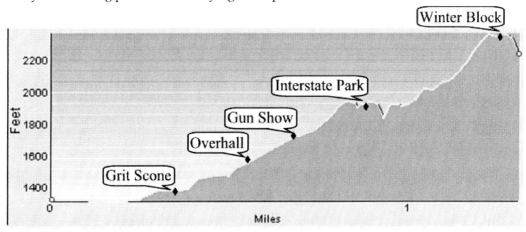

Wall Difficulty

The graph below shows the general route difficulty of each wall. For example, if you're an advanced climber (5.11+), then head to Overhaul; if you're just getting started (5.6+), then Gritscone and Interstate Park are choice destinations.

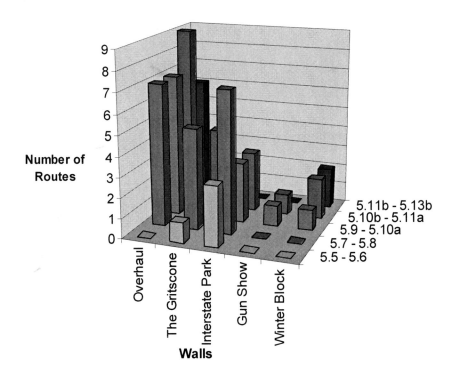

We are ne'er like angels till our passion dies.
 ¯Thomas Dekker

Getting to Far Side

To reach the Far Side parking area take Exit 38 off Interstate 90 and follow the paved Exit 38 road for two miles. The parking area is just past the Interstate 90 overpass.

For some reason, people feel compelled to dispose of their unwanted items at this parking area. I'm not sure why but I believe it has something to do with the high voltage power lines which are directly overhead. My theory is they exert an intense electromagnetic field which negatively influences the Neuroglial cells in the Cerebellum causing people to subconsciously throw things from their vehicles. Of course, I might be wrong but it supports my optimistic view that all people are noble and above such disgraceful deeds.

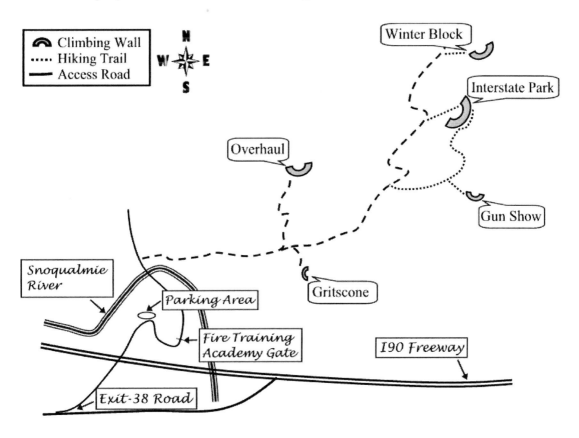

Parking

Unlike the luxurious Deception Crags climbing area (which has a large parking area, instructional signs, informational bulletin boards, deluxe toilets.) Far Side simply offers parking at the side of the road. The good news is it's near a high voltage power line which does a fantastic job of reducing the bug population in the summer time.

Hiking Trail

From the parking area, hike four minutes (400 yards) on the continued paved State Fire Training Center road until you reach a bridge over the Snoqualmie River. The hiking trail starts just after you cross the bridge on the right side of the road. It follows the river for a few hundred meters and then angles up the old Pacific Western Telephone & Telegraph trail.

Overhaul Wall

Overhaul Wall is a long wall divided into three climbing sections: Relief Camp, Motherland, and Slabbage Patch.

The lower portion of the wall, Relief Camp, has mostly 5.10a – 5.11a level routes on a slightly inverted face. It has the unique characteristic of being half shade (in the trees) and half sun (above the trees). The middle section, Motherland, offers a wide rage of climbing difficulty. It receives the most sun and is a great place for early spring and fall climbing. If you're just getting into the sport of rock climbing, then the upper portion of the wall, Slabbage Patch, offers several excellent 5.7-5.9 level routes.

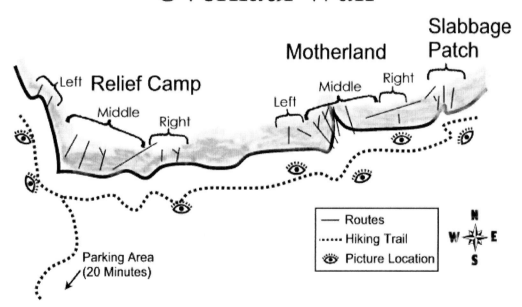

Getting to Overhaul

To reach Overhaul, hike up the main trail from the parking area for 15 minutes (.7 miles) and take the first side trail to the left (the right side trail leads to Gritscone, Squishy Bell, and Winter Block). Continue on this trail for another 5 minutes (.4 miles to the lower left section of Overhaul). See the mape on page 175 for more information.

Notes _____

_____

_____

_____

_____

_____

_____

_____

_____

_____

_____

_____

_____

_____

_____

_____

_____

_____ **Date** _____

Difficulty	Route	Bolts	Rating	Top Rope	Route Name	Stats	
5.12b	A	5	★	No	Ghost p. 233	☐ Lead ☐ Top Rope	☐ Redpoint ☐ Flash
5.12c	B	6	★	No	Green Lantern p. 233	☐ Lead ☐ Top Rope	☐ Redpoint ☐ Flash

Notes _____

_____

_____

_____

_____

_____

_____

_____

_____

_____

_____

_____

_____

_____

_____

_____

_____

_____

_____

_____

_____

_____

_____ **Date** _____

Difficulty	Route	Bolts	Rating	Top Rope	Route Name	Stats	
5.11b	C	9	★★	No	Complete Overhaul p. 232	□ Lead □ Top Rope	□ Redpoint □ Flash
5.8	D	3	★★	No	Chain Gain p. 228	□ Lead □ Top Rope	□ Redpoint □ Flash
5.10d	E	10	★★★	No	Mr. Fixit p. 231	□ Lead □ Top Rope	□ Redpoint □ Flash
5.11b	F	10	★★★	No	Chain Gang p. 231	□ Lead □ Top Rope	□ Redpoint □ Flash
5.10a	G	4	★★	No	Shelf Serve p. 230	□ Lead □ Top Rope	□ Redpoint □ Flash

The Edge
It's a bridge
It's unquestionable faith
It's pure potential
It's perfect balance

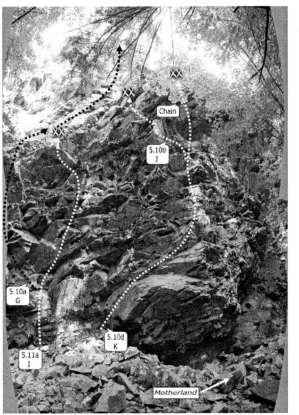

Notes _____

_____

_____

_____

_____

_____

_____

_____

_____

_____

_____

_____

_____

_____ **Date** _____

Difficulty	Route	Bolts	Rating	Top Rope	Route Name	Stats	
5.10a	G	11	★★★	No	Rhino Relief p. 229	□ Lead □ Top Rope	□ Redpoint □ Flash
5.11a	I	0	★★★	No	Give Until It Hurts p. 232	□ Lead □ Top Rope	□ Redpoint □ Flash
5.10b	J	6	★	No	Controlled Bleeding p. 230	□ Lead □ Top Rope	□ Redpoint □ Flash
5.10d	K	6	★★★	No	Jugular Vein p. 231	□ Lead □ Top Rope	□ Redpoint □ Flash

Notes _____

_____

_____

_____

_____

_____

_____

_____

_____

_____

_____

_____

_____

_____

_____

_____**Date**_____

Difficulty	Route	Bolts	Rating	Top Rope	Route Name	Stats	
5.12b	A	4	★	No	Flubber p. 233	□ Lead □ Top Rope	□ Redpoint □ Flash
5.7	B	4	★ ★	No	False Pretenses p. 225	□ Lead □ Top Rope	□ Redpoint □ Flash

Difficulty	Route	Bolts	Rating	Top Rope	Route Name	Stats	
5.7	B	4	★★	No	False Pretenses p. 226	□ Lead □ Top Rope	□ Redpoint □ Flash
5.8	C	4	★★	No	Cornery Bypass p. 228	□ Lead □ Top Rope	□ Redpoint □ Flash
5.8	D	4	★★	No	Corner's Inquest p. 228	□ Lead □ Top Rope	□ Redpoint □ Flash
5.10a	E	6	★★	No	Toying With My Affections p. 229	□ Lead □ Top Rope	□ Redpoint □ Flash
5.10b	F	7	★★	No	Toying With My Afflictions p. 230	□ Lead □ Top Rope	□ Redpoint □ Flash
5.11a	G	7	★★	No	Foreplay p. 232	□ Lead □ Top Rope	□ Redpoint □ Flash
5.10b	H	7	★★★	No	Sheltered Upbringing p. 230	□ Lead □ Top Rope	□ Redpoint □ Flash
5.11a	I	9	★★★	No	Moreplay ! See Beta p. 232	□ Lead □ Top Rope	□ Redpoint □ Flash
5.12b	J	6	★★★	No	Hovering Mother p. 233	□ Lead □ Top Rope	□ Redpoint □ Flash
5.12b	K	6	★★★	No	Offspring p. 233	□ Lead □ Top Rope	□ Redpoint □ Flash
5.8	L	8	★★	No	On The Outskirts ! See Beta p. 227	□ Lead □ Top Rope	□ Redpoint □ Flash

Notes _____

_____

_____   *Date*_____

Notes _____

_____

_____

_____

_____

_____

_____

_____

_____

_____

_____

_____

_____

_____

_____

_____

_____ **Date** _____

Difficulty	Route	Bolts	Rating	Top Rope	Route Name	Stats	
5.8	L	7	★★	No	On the Outskirts p. 227	□ Lead □ Top Rope	□ Redpoint □ Flash
5.10d	M	3	★★	No	Stretcher Case p. 231	□ Lead □ Top Rope	□ Redpoint □ Flash

Kim making the move on
Chain Gang – 5.11b (p.182)

Difficulty	Route	Bolts	Rating	Top Rope	Route Name	Stats	
5.9	A	13	★★	No	End Run ! See Beta p. 228	□ Lead □ Top Rope	□ Redpoint □ Flash
5.9	C	7	★★★	No	Siamese Dream p. 228	□ Lead □ Top Rope	□ Redpoint □ Flash
5.9	D	4	★	No	Nature Boy p. 229	□ Lead □ Top Rope	□ Redpoint □ Flash
5.7	E	5	★★	No	Party Girl p. 226	□ Lead □ Top Rope	□ Redpoint □ Flash

Notes _____

_____

_____

_____

_____

_____**Date** _____

> The hand trembles. The body tenses.
> An unquestionable instant of alarm.
>
> Honor the body's warnings... **reach and believe.**

Gritscone

Gritscone is a chunk of conglomerate sandstone deposited in a terminal moraine during the last ice age about 12,000 years ago. Translation - it's a big rock. If you're just learning how to rock climb this is a great place to visit. The routes are short (four bolts or less), easily top roped, and mostly between 5.5 - 5.9.

The upper left portion of the rock has a uniquely course texture which makes for some interesting slab climbing and, if you're not careful, quick skin removal. The left section is steeper but with big, reassuring hand holds. The middle section is slightly overhanging with the most difficult route (5.11d) on the rock. The right side offers several short beginning level routes.

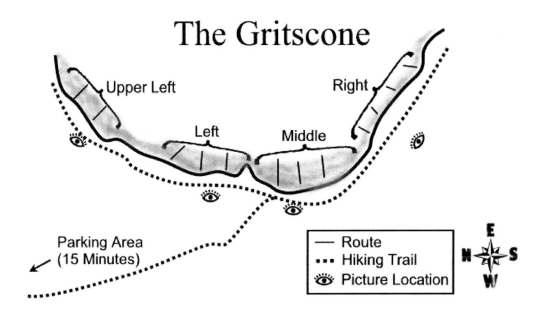

The Gritscone

Upper Left   Right

Left   Middle

Parking Area
(15 Minutes)

| — Route |
| ••• Hiking Trail |
| 👁 Picture Location |

To reach Gritscone, follow the main trail from the parking lot for 15 minutes (.7 miles) and take the right side trail. Follow this side trail for 60 meters to the lower left section of the wall. See the map on page 175 for more information.

Difficulty	Route	Bolts	Rating	Top Rope	Route Name	Stats	
5.7	A	3	★★	✓	Needle Magnet p. 225	□ Lead □ Top Rope	□ Redpoint □ Flash
5.9	B	2	★★	✓	Magnetic Anomaly p. 229	□ Lead □ Top Rope	□ Redpoint □ Flash

Notes _____

_____ *Date* _____

Difficulty	Route	Bolts	Rating	Top Rope	Route Name	Stats	
5.6	C	3	★★	✓	Lucky Arms p. 225	□ Lead □ Top Rope	□ Redpoint □ Flash
5.7	D	2	★★	✓	Snaffle Baffler p. 225	□ Lead □ Top Rope	□ Redpoint □ Flash
5.11d	E	3	★★	No	Rough Cut p. 232	□ Lead □ Top Rope	□ Redpoint □ Flash

Notes _____

_____ *Date* _____

Difficulty	Route	Bolts	Rating	Top Rope	Route Name	Stats	
5.11d	E	3	★★	No	Rough Cut p. 232	□ Lead □ Top Rope	□ Redpoint □ Flash
5.11a	F	3	★★	✓	A Girl's Best Friend p. 232	□ Lead □ Top Rope	□ Redpoint □ Flash
5.10c	G	3	★★	✓	Booty Squirrel p. 231	□ Lead □ Top Rope	□ Redpoint □ Flash
5.10a	H	4	★★★	✓	Chica Rapida p. 229	□ Lead □ Top Rope	□ Redpoint □ Flash

Notes _____

_____ *Date* _____

Difficulty	Route	Bolts	Rating	Top Rope	Route Name	Stats	
5.9	I	3	★★★	✓	99 Grit p. 228	☐ Lead ☐ Top Rope	☐ Redpoint ☐ Flash
5.7	J	3	★★★	✓	Pete's Possum Palace p. 225	☐ Lead ☐ Top Rope	☐ Redpoint ☐ Flash
5.7	K	2	★★	✓	So Funny I Forgot To Rope Up p. 225	☐ Lead ☐ Top Rope	☐ Redpoint ☐ Flash
5.5	L	2	★★	✓	So Easy I Forgot To Laugh p. 225	☐ Lead ☐ Top Rope	☐ Redpoint ☐ Flash

Notes _____

_____ *Date* _____

Gun Show

Gun Show is a large slab below Interstate Park which has two sport routes. The left route is a super 40 meter 5.10a slab that is the best in the area. The route on the right side is a short but intertesting "wedgie" route. It's best if you have a climbing plan when you start these routes because the freeway noise is so loud you will not be able to hear each other past the 8th bolt.

Several new routes are being worked on in this area so check the web site www.northbendrock.com for the most recent route information.

The Gun Show gets its name from… actually, it would be more interesting if you discovered that one on your own. ☺

To reach Gun Show continue hiking for 5 minutes up the main trail past the side trail to Gritscone (.23 miles) and take the obvious side trail to the right.

Follow this trail for 5 minutes to another side trail to the right. Hike for 3 minutes down this trail to the base of the Gun Show wall. (See the map on page 175 for details.)

The Gun Show

Notes _____

_____

_____

_____

_____

_____

_____

_____

_____

_____

_____

_____

_____

_____

_____

_____

_____ **Date** _____

Difficulty	Route	Bolts	Rating	Top Rope	Route Name	Stats	
5.10a	A	16	★★★★	No	Endless Bliss p. 229	□ Lead □ Top Rope	□ Redpoint □ Flash
5.10d	B	4	★★	No	Super Squish p. 231	□ Lead □ Top Rope	□ Redpoint □ Flash

Beth catching a helpful updraft on
Endless Bliss – 5.10a (p. 199)
(Photo By Dave Argento)

Interstate Park Far Side

Interstate Park is a band of rock 20 meters high and 150 meters wide just to the North of the I-90 freeway. It's the newest addition to the areas sport climbing collection which continues the Exit 38 tradition of larger than life holds on a vertical wall. Because it's a recent development the routes tend to be less crowded so make sure you wear your brain bucket because there is potentially more lose rock than the other well traveled areas.

Interstate Park has three distinct sections; Squishy Bell, Eastern Block, and Headlight Point. It has some of the best 5.6 – 5.9 climbing in the valley. Because of its southern expose it enjoys lots of year round sun which makes it ideal for spring and fall climbing.

Note: There are several crags by Interstate Park which may be developed in the future. Check http://www.northbendrock.com for the latest route information.

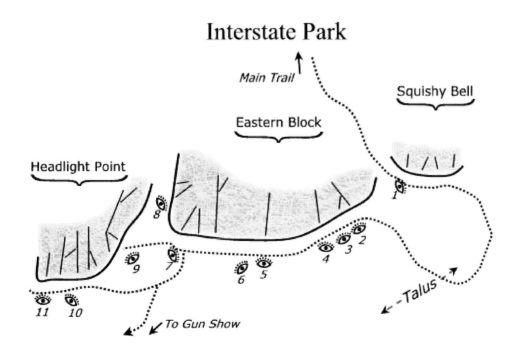

This picture is taken from the ridge across the talus slope just to the east of Interstate Park.

Eastern Block

Squishy Bell

Headlight Point

It is a happy talent to know how to play.
-Ralph Waldo Emerson

The happiest talent is to know how to play with yourself.
-Eric Cartman

To reach Interstate Park take the first side trail to the right past Gritscone (see map on page 175). Follow it for 15 minutes down and around the ridge to the bottom of the wall.

Note: About 7 minutes after taking a right off of the main trail you'll see the turn off to Gun Show. Continue straight and hike up the ridge another 7 minutes to a small clearing overlooking Interstate 90. This is the bottom of the Headlight Point section of Interstate Park.

Squishy Bell

Squishy Bell is the smallest of the three walls on the right side of Interstate Park. It has four petite routes from 5.5 – 5.9.

One of the pleasant thing about Squishy Bell is the routes can easily be top roped. This means that if you can't afford draws, or just don't want to be over burdened with the extra 2.5 pounds of weight, you can still enjoy some rock climbing. To reach the chains simply hike up the left side and around to the top.

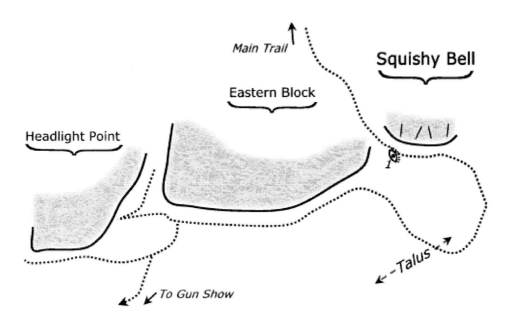

> Only passions, great passions, can elevate the soul to
> great things.   -Diderot

Squishy Belll

Difficulty	Route	Bolts	Rating	Top Rope	Route Name	Stats	
5.6	A	2	★★	✓	Catatonic p. 225	□ Lead □ Top Rope	□ Redpoint □ Flash
5.8	B	4	★★	✓	Winter Rushing In p. 228	□ Lead □ Top Rope	□ Redpoint □ Flash
5.9	C	4	★★★	✓	November Glaze p. 229	□ Lead □ Top Rope	□ Redpoint □ Flash
5.5	D	2	★★	✓	Sumptuous Bits p. 225	□ Lead □ Top Rope	□ Redpoint □ Flash

Eastern Block

Eastern Block is the major rock wall between Squishy Bell and Headlight Point. The entire wall is a unique series of interwoven blocks which make for some of the most amazing jug climbing your ever likely to encounter.

The right section of the wall is nearly vertical but because of the plethora of monster jugs its difficulty is around 5.7 – 5.9. The middle section is overhanging with a grand roof at the top of wall but again, because of those wonderfully fat holds, the most difficult route is 5.11a.

The left side of the Eastern Block has a couple of unique climbs in what's affectionately refered to as "The Cave of Doom". Step into the cave and look up and you'll quickly understand the name and contemplate your mortality. The route at the back of cave is way cool - you actually have to squeeze through a hole at the top of the cave to finish it.

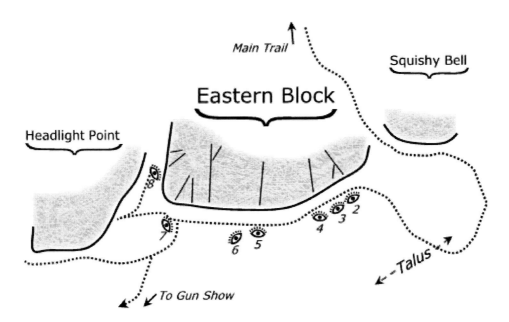

Notes _____

_____

_____

_____

_____

_____

_____

_____

_____

_____

_____

_____

_____

_____

_____

_____

_____

_____ **Date** _____

Difficulty	Route	Bolts	Rating	Top Rope	Route Name	Stats	
5.7	I	7	★★★	No	Kiss Of The Crowbar p. 225	□ Lead □ Top Rope	□ Redpoint □ Flash

Notes _____

_____

_____

_____

_____

_____

_____

_____

_____

_____

_____

_____

_____

_____

_____

_____

_____ **Date** _____

Difficulty	Route	Bolts	Rating	Top Rope	Route Name	Stats	
5.10b	G	8	★★★	No	Missing The Taco p. 230	☐ Lead ☐ Top Rope	☐ Redpoint ☐ Flash
5.8	H	8	★★★	No	Attack Of The Butter Knives p. 227	☐ Lead ☐ Top Rope	☐ Redpoint ☐ Flash
5.7	I	7	★★★	No	Kiss Of The Crowbar p. 225	☐ Lead ☐ Top Rope	☐ Redpoint ☐ Flash

5.10b
G

Difficulty	Route	Bolts	Rating	Top Rope	Route Name	Stats	
5.10b	G	8	★★★	No	Missing The Taco p. 225	☐ Lead ☐ Top Rope	☐ Redpoint ☐ Flash

Notes _____

_____

_____

_____ **Date** _____

Author floating up
Space Face – 5.10d (p. 213)
(Photo By Dave Argento)

Deceased Tree

XX

5.10a
F

Headlight Point

Squishy Bell

Notes _____

_____

_____

_____

_____

_____

_____

_____

_____

_____

_____

_____

_____

_____

_____

_____

_____

_____

_____

_____

_____

_____

___**Date** _____

Difficulty	Route	Bolts	Rating	Top Rope	Route Name	Stats	
5.10a	F	6	★★★	No	Ellie's Sweet Kiss p. 225	□ Lead □ Top Rope	□ Redpoint □ Flash

Notes _____

_____

_____

_____

_____

_____

_____

_____

_____

_____

_____

_____

_____

_____

_____

_____

_____

_____

_____

_____ **Date** _____

Difficulty	Route	Bolts	Rating	Top Rope	Route Name	Stats	
5.11a	E	9	★★★	No	Strategic Placement p. 225	□ Lead □ Top Rope	□ Redpoint □ Flash
5.10d	D	9	★★★	No	Displacement p. 225	□ Lead □ Top Rope	□ Redpoint □ Flash

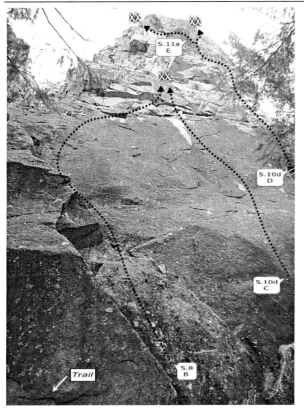

Notes _____

_____

_____

_____

_____

_____

_____

_____

_____

_____

_____

_____

_____

_____**Date** _____

Difficulty	Route	Bolts	Rating	Top Rope	Route Name	Stats		
5.8	B	6	★★★	No	Impartial Eclipse p. 227	□ Lead □ Top Rope	□ Redpoint □ Flash	
5.10d	C	6	★★★	No	Space Face p. 231	□ Lead □ Top Rope	□ Redpoint □ Flash	
5.10d	D	9	★★★	No	Displacement p. 231	□ Lead □ Top Rope	□ Redpoint □ Flash	
5.11a	E	9	★★★	No	Strategic Placement p. 232	□ Lead □ Top Rope	□ Redpoint □ Flash	

Notes _____

_____ **Date** _____

Difficulty	Route	Bolts	Rating	Top Rope	Route Name	Stats		
5.8	A	5	★★★	No	Tunnel Of Love p. 227	□ Lead □ Top Rope	□ Redpoint □ Flash	
5.10b	B	6	★★★	No	Lip Service p. 231	□ Lead □ Top Rope	□ Redpoint □ Flash	

Author indulging himself on
Lip Service – 5.10b (p.214)
(Photo By Chris Madden)

Headlight point is the left (southern) section of the Interstate Park area. Similar to Eastern Block, it has astonishing jugs but on a moderate incline which yields the best 5.6 – 5.8 routes in the valley.

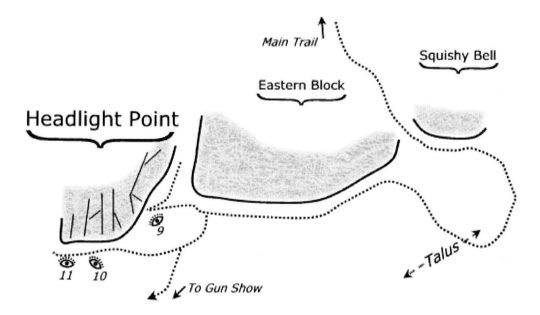

Life shrinks and expands in proportion to one's courage.
— *Anais Nin*

Difficulty	Route	Bolts	Rating	Top Rope	Route Name	Stats	
5.6	H	3	★★★	No	Eating Rocks p. 226	□ Lead □ Top Rope	□ Redpoint □ Flash
5.6	I	3	★★★	No	Eating Dust p. 225	□ Lead □ Top Rope	□ Redpoint □ Flash
5.8	J	10	★★★	No	Insomniac p.227	□ Lead □ Top Rope	□ Redpoint □ Flash
5.10b	K	5 (Pro to 3 ")	★★★	No	Bicycling To Bellingham ! See Beta p. 230	□ Lead □ Top Rope	□ Redpoint □ Flash

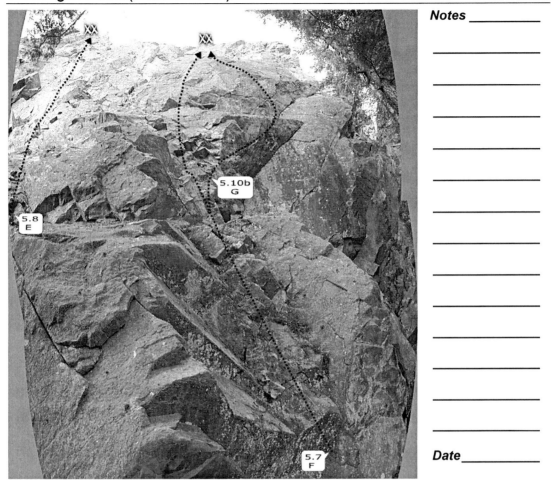

Notes _____

_____

_____

_____

_____

_____

_____

_____

_____

_____

_____

_____

_____

_____

_____

Date _____

Difficulty	Route	Bolts	Rating	Top Rope	Route Name	Stats	
5.8	E	6	★★★	No	Nocturnal Remission p. 227	□ Lead □ Top Rope	□ Redpoint □ Flash
5.7	F	5	★★★	No	Swarm p. 226	□ Lead □ Top Rope	□ Redpoint □ Flash
5.10b	G	6	★★★	No	Carnage Before Bedtime p. 230	□ Lead □ Top Rope	□ Redpoint □ Flash

Notes _____

_____

_____

_____

_____

_____

_____

_____

_____

_____

_____

_____

_____ **Date** _____

Difficulty	Route	Bolts	Rating	Top Rope	Route Name	Stats	
5.7	A	3	★★★	No	Swerve p. 226	□ Lead □ Top Rope	□ Redpoint □ Flash
5.6	B	2	★★★	No	In The Middle Again p. 225	□ Lead □ Top Rope	□ Redpoint □ Flash
5.7	C	4	★★★	No	Midnight Scrambler p. 226	□ Lead □ Top Rope	□ Redpoint □ Flash
5.8	D	4	★★★	No	Light-Headed Again p. 227	□ Lead □ Top Rope	□ Redpoint □ Flash

Curtis Beach finding himself
In The Middle Again - 5.6 (p. 219)

Winter Block

If you're into flying kites and climbing, this could be your wall of nirvana. At 2373 feet elevation, Winter Block is the most distant and the highest crag in the Far Side area. Like Squishy Bell, it faces southeast on the ridge line for splendid views of McClellan's Butte and the modern concrete trail, referred to as Interstate 90, to the South.

Of all the walls at Far Side Winter Block gets the fewest visitors. Reason – there only four routes mostly in the range of 5.10 – 5.11 and it's a moderate 35 minute hike. So, if you're a climber who likes a little solitude, head on up and if you don't get the pump you need stop by Interstate Park on the way down.

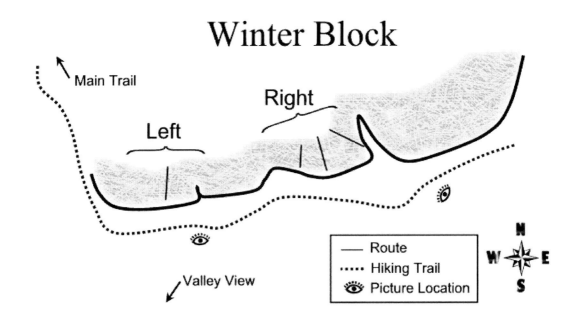

To get to Winter Block, continue on the main trail another 15 minutes (.8 mile) and take the side trail to the right. Hike across the ridge 100 meters on the side trail to the upper left section of the crag. To reach the bottom, follow the trail down a short hill along the edge of the crag and let the fun begin.

Note: After hiking 5 minutes past the side trail to Gun Show and Interstate Park you will pass another side trial to the right. This trail leads to the top of Squishy Bell in Interstate Park. Continue past it another 10 minutes to reach the side trail to Winter Block shown above.

Winter Block (Left)

_____

_____

_____

_____

_____

_____

_____

_____

_____

_____

_____

_____

_____

_____

_____

_____

_____Date _____

Difficulty	Route	Bolts	Rating	Top Rope	Route Name	Stats		
5.10d	A	3	★★	No	Seismic Mardi Gras p. 231	□ Lead □ Top Rope	□ Redpoint □ Flash	

_____

_____

_____

_____

_____

_____

_____

_____

_____

_____

_____

_____

_____ **Date** _____

Difficulty	Route	Bolts	Rating	Top Rope	Route Name	Stats	
5.12+	B	-	-	No	(Project)	☐ Lead ☐ Top Rope	☐ Redpoint ☐ Flash
5.11b	C	5	★★	No	Of Gossamer Shrouds p. 232	☐ Lead ☐ Top Rope	☐ Redpoint ☐ Flash
5.10c	D	6	★★★	No	Winter Walk Within p. 231	☐ Lead ☐ Top Rope	☐ Redpoint ☐ Flash
5.9	E	4	★★★	✓	And The Sun Will Never Rise Again p. 229	☐ Lead ☐ Top Rope	☐ Redpoint ☐ Flash

Far Side Route Listings

Difficulty	Route Name	Rating	Area	Wall	Beta
5.5	So Easy I forgot to Laugh p. 195	★ ★	Far Side	Gritscone	A great route the whole family (including your dog) can enjoy. –Garth Bruce FA: Bryan Burdo, Sarah Leonard 10/99
	Sumptuous Bits p. 205	★ ★	Far Side	Squishy Bell	A generous helping of heaping holds with a top rope option make this a good route for beginners. –Garth Bruce FA: Steve Martin, Jeff Forister & Carrie Akerstrom
5.6	Eating Dust p. 217	★ ★ ★	Far Side	Interstate Park	One of two virtually identical routes joined at the chain. Also a good warm up for a fun 5.8 that follow them up the arête. –Garth Bruce FA: Bryan Burdo 7/02
	Eating Rocks p. 217	★ ★ ★	Far Side	Headlight Point	Fortunately, all the rocks are gone on the route now so your belay won't have to worry about eating any more. –Garth Bruce FA: Bryan Burdo 7/02
	In The Middle Again p. 219	★ ★ ★	Far Side	Headlight Point	Climb first two bolts and then head right via slab to finish at "Light-Headed Again" Anchors. FA: Bryan Burdo 7/02
	Lucky Arms p. 193	★ ★	Far Side	Gritscone	Your arms, legs, knees, and elbows can all get lucky and enjoy this route. –Garth Bruce FA: Bryan Burdo, Leland Windham, Sarah Leonard 10/99
	Catatonic p. 205	★ ★	Far Side	Squishy Bell	A quickie two bolt route on the squishy end of Squishy Bell. –Garth Bruce FA: Jeff Forister & Carrie Akerstrom
5.7	Kiss Of The Crowbar p. 207	★ ★ ★	Far Side	Eastern Block	A beautiful route with the biggest and best jugs in the valley. –Garth Bruce FA: Bryan Burdo 7/02

iculty	Route Name	Rating	Area	Wall	Beta
	Swerve p. 219	★ ★ ★	Far Side	Headlight Point	No need to swerve off of this route – it's straight and solid to the chains going up and coming down. –Garth Bruce FA: Bryan Burdo 7/02
	Swarm p. 217	★ ★ ★	Far Side	Headlight Point	Stamp on some easy ramp as "Carnage". Keep going left until clear of the overhang then head straight up on the jugs. –Bryan Burdo FA: Bryan Burdo 7/02
	Midnight Scrambler p. 219	★ ★ ★	Far Side	Headlight Point	An optional finish on the route "In the Middle Again". Just after the first bolt you'll notice two bolts a few feet from each other. Clip the left one and continue up and left. –Garth Bruce FA: Bryan Burdo 7/02
	Pete's Possum Palace p. 195	★ ★ ★	Far Side	Gritscone	If you like to sleep with Possums climb this route and then call Pete for reservations. –Garth Bruce FA: Bryan Burdo, Leland Windham, Sarah Leonard10/99
	Party Girl p. 186	★ ★	Far Side	Slabbage Patch	She used to be kind of loose but now she's just fun to be with. –Bryan Burdo FA: Bryan Burdo
	Needle Magnet p. 192	★ ★	Far Side	Gritscone	A short slabbish route on a super grip surface. For the best climb experience I suggest you vacuum the route first. –Garth Bruce FA: Bryan Burdo, Leland Windham, Sarah Leonard10/99
	So Funny I Forgot To Rope Up p. 195	★ ★	Far Side	Gritscone	So funny I forgot to writeup beta. –Garth Bruce FA: Bryan Burdo, Leland Windham, Sarah Leonard10/99
	False Pretense p. 184	★ ★	Far Side	Motherland	Acrophobes need not apply! Not really a good beginner's route due to the exposed lower-off. –Bryan Burdo FA: Bryan Burdo

Difficulty	Route Name	Rating	Area	Wall	Beta
	Snaffle Baffler p. 193	★★	Far Side	Gritscone	A bit snaffily at the end but it has an enjoyable start. –Garth Bruce FA: Bryan Burdo, Leland Windham, Sarah Leonard 10/99
5.8	Attack Of The Butter Knives p. 207	★★★	Far Side	Eastern Block	At the first large ledge, continue right to finish on "Crowbar" or left on a slab to finish on the upper face of "Taco". –Bryan Burdo FA: Bryan Burdo 06/02
	Insomniac p. 217	★★★	Far Side	Headlight Point	Climb the clean dihedral right of the crack and finish on the classic arête to the chains. –Bryan Burdo FA: Bryan Burdo 06/02
	Nocturnal Remission p. 218	★★★	Far Side	Eastern Block	This route name could have been "Nocturnal Emission" because it left me exhausted but satisfied after I climbed it. –Garth Bruce FA: Bryan Burdo 06/02
	Tunnel Of Love p. 214	★★★	Far Side	Eastern Block	Garth didn't like my route name "Delightful Cacoffiny Funnelled Within" so he named it "Tunnel Of Love" – Leland Windham FA: Leland Windham, Garth Bruce 07/02
	Impartial Eclipse p. 213	★★★	Far Side	Eastern Block	Follow the mini ramp up and left then veer right to a ledge and up to the chains. FA: Bryan Burdo 05/02
	Light-Headed Again p. 219	★★★	Far Side	Headlight Point	The picture shows this route starting up straight and then curving to the left. Not true. It continues straight to the top. –Garth Bruce FA: Bryan Burdo 05/02
	On The Outskirts p. 184	★★	Far Side	Slabbage Patch	Sidles along the slabs beneath the cave to an anchor at its upper right-hand extremity. Low-angle climbing with high exposure. To descend, be prepared to land well on up the trail, or use the "Trolley" method of descent. –Bryan Burdo FA: Bryan Burdo

Difficulty	Route Name	Rating	Area	Wall	Beta
	Winter Rushing In p. 205	★★	Far Side	Squishy Bell	Textured jugs angling rightward up the center of the slab. – Leland Windham FA: Leland Windham & Steve Martin 11/00
	Chain Gain p. 179	★★	Far Side	Relief Camp	Ends at "Chain Ledge." Climbs the initial arête to the bug ledge. –Bryan Burdo FA: Bryan Burdo
	Cornery Bypass p. 184	★★	Far Side	Motherland	Begin along False Pretenses and ascend the arête to "Inquest' anchor. –Bryan Burdo FA: Bryan Burdo
	Corner's Inquest p. 184	★★	Far Side	Motherland	Look what we dug up! Inch for inch the cleaning challenge of the decade, but things turned out just fine. –Bryan Burdo FA: Bryan Burdo
5.9	Endrun p. 184	★★★	Far Side	Motherland	Continue the adventure on the fine, gritty rock to the top of the crag for an alpine like pitch with great protection. Rope drag is a factor, so use long runners and unclip early bolts to ensure a safe and pleasant final rappel to the base of "Siamese Dream". –Bryan Burdo FA: Bryan Burdo
	Endrun Direct p. 186	★★★	Far Side	Slabbage Patch	From a small arête left of "Stretcher Case" slab, climb directly to gain the ledge below the "Mother Cave." Use long runners. Stays drier than original start. –Bryan Burdo FA: Bryan Burdo
	Siamese Dream p. 186	★★★	Far Side	Slabbage Patch	Probably the sunniest exposure of any route in this guide with some great rock and variety of moves to make this one rather smashing. Two starts (either left with the arête or right with the crack) are "joined at the bolt." Finishing via "Outskirts" is a bit easier. –Bryan Burdo FA: Bryan Burdo
	99 Grit p. 195	★★★	Far Side	Gritscone	A gripping route straight up the face. –Garth Bruce FA: Bryan Burdo

Difficulty	Route Name	Rating	Area	Wall	Beta
	And The Sun Will Never Rise Again p. 223	★ ★ ★	Far Side	Winter Block	A lustrous sun-baked slab rising from nocturnal grit supreme. –Leland Windham FA: Leland Windham, Jeff Forister & Steve Martin 5/01
	November Glaze p. 205	★ ★ ★	Far Side	Squishy Bell	Small roof to short slab. Coated in super grit. –Leland Windham FA: Leland Windham & Steve Martin 11/00
	Magnetic Anomaly p. 192	★ ★	Far Side	Gritscone	Don't slip on this route or the large patches of skin missing on your body will be the anomaly. –Garth Bruce FA: Bryan Burdo
	Nature Boy p. 186	★	Far Side	Slabbage Patch	This guy is a bit crude, but has good potential once he has been properly cleaned up. Stem the tricky corner. –Bryan Burdo FA: Bryan Burdo
5.10a	Endless Bliss p. 199	★ ★ ★ ★	Far Side	Gun Show	135 feet of prodigious slab climbing equipped with a midway anchor so you can get down with one rope. The traffic noise and gun fire makes communicating with your belayer a little annoying but the climbing is so good that I almost forgot to mention that. –Leland Windham FA: Leland Windham, Dave Wolfe
	Ellie's Sweet Kiss p. 211	★ ★ ★	Far Side	Eastern Block	Feel the joy of this rewarding route which just gets better and better as your journey continues. FA: Garth Bruce, Leland Windham, Bryan Burdo 6/02
	Chica Rapida p. 194	★ ★ ★	Far Side	Gritscone	She is so fine and delightful to climb so take your time and enjoy her. –Garth Bruce FA: Bryan Burdo, Sarah Lenard
	Rhino Relief p. 182	★ ★ ★	Far Side	Overhaul	! The safest start option is to stick-clip the first bolt (above the massive suspicious block), then start from the right on "Give Until It Hurts" and moving left. Long runners useful. –Bryan Burdo FA: Bryan Burdo

Difficulty	Route Name	Rating	Area	Wall	Beta
	Shelf Serve p. 182	★★	Far Side	Overhaul	A small climb with some huge holds. –Bryan Burdo FA: Bryan Brudo
	Toying With My Affections p. 184	★★	Far Side	Motherland	Start via "Inquest" and proceed up the left side of the face past two small overhangs. –Bryan Burdo FA: Bryan Burdo
5.10b	Missing The Taco p. 208	★★★	Far Side	Eastern Block	A bit devious at the start. –Bryan Burdo FA: Bryan Burdo, Dave Wolfe
	Bicycling To Bellingham p. 217	★★★	Far Side	Headlight Point	Start using the left hand option of "Insomniac". Climb the perfect 25' handcrack (5.7) to the arête. Climb up a few bolts and exit right to the easy 3" crack. Follow it up to the roof and esxit right to a bolt and the crux move into the final alcove. –Bryan Burdo FA: Bryan Burdo
	Carnage Before Bedtime p. 218	★★★	Far Side	Headlight Point	An interesting side-steppin underclingin deviation from the Swarm route. –Garth Bruce FA: Bryan Burdo
	Sheltered Upbringing p. 184	★★★	Far Side	Motherland	Fondle your way up this face, with a dramatic exit on the left side of the "Mother" roof. –Bryan Burdo FA: Bryan Burdo
	Lip Service p. 214	★★★	Far Side	Eastern Block	Leland didn't like my name "Kiss Me Before You Climb Me" so I changed it to "Lip Service". –Garth Bruce FA: Garth Bruce, Leland Windham 7/02
	Toying With My Afflictions (Variation) p. 184	★★	Far Side	Motherland	Starts via "Foreplay." –Bryan Burdo FA: Bryan Burdo
	Controlled Bleeding p. 182	★	Far Side	Overhaul	Exits left before things get too critical. –Bryan Burdo FA: Bryan Burdo

Difficulty	Route Name	Rating	Area	Wall	Beta
5.10c	Mr. FixIt p. 179	★ ★ ★	Far Side	Relief Camp	This is the easiest foray on the left side of the wall, beginning on Chain Gain or Shelf. –Bryan Burdo FA: Bryan Burdo
	Winter Walk Within p. 223	★ ★ ★	Far Side	Winter Block	Wander up the semi-floppy chimney then step right and attack the arête above. –Leland Windham FA: Leland Windham & Steve Martin 07/01
	Booty Squirrel p. 194	★ ★	Far Side	Gritscone	All the holds you need are there without a lot of extra one to confuse you. Note: Nuts not required. –Garth Bruce. FA: Bryan Burdo 10/99
5.10d	Displacement p. 212	★ ★ ★	Far Side	Eastern Block	At the final ledge just under the roof go up and right to the bottom of the roof. Take a moment to pray you don't falter and pendulum into next week, then pull the lip. –Garth Bruce FA: Bryan Burdo, Garth Bruce
	Jugular Vein p. 182	★ ★ ★	Far Side	Relief Camp	Climb up weirdness to some high drama. Once you know the beta it's significantly easier. –Bryan Burdo FA: Bryan Burdo
	Space Face p. 213	★ ★ ★	Far Side	Eastern Block	Eastern Block is jug city and then there is this anomaly. Micro edges on a short steep slab. One of my favorites. –Garth Bruce FA: Bryan Burdo
	Super Squish p. 197	★ ★	Far Side	Gun Show	Squish yourself into this unique shallow corner for a short series of bizarre squirming, palming, smearing and edging on some extremely sticky rock. –Leland Windham FA: Leland Windham, Dave Wolfe 5/02
	Seismic Mardi Gras p. 223	★ ★	Far Side	Winter Block	A rumbling party. Put up during the earthquake of 2001. –Leland Windham FA: Jeff Forister, Carrie Akerstrom & Leland Windham 05/01
	Stretcher Case p. 186	★ ★	Far Side	Slabbage Patch	Short and "gymmy" on unique rock. –Bryan Burdo FA: Bryan Burdo

Difficulty	Route Name	Rating	Area	Wall	Beta
5.11a	Strategic Placement p. 212	★ ★ ★	Far Side	Eastern Block	Nice crack at the beginning of this route which can take an optional ½ " nut or 1 ½ " cam by the second bolt. Grope for a pocket at the crux on the roof lip – if you can't find it veer left for an easier finish. –Garth Bruce FA: Bryan Burdo
	Moreplay p. 184	★ ★ ★	Far Side	Motherland	2 bolt extension of Foreplay or Sheltered Upbringing (use long runners on last two bolts of "Upbringing" if you use it). The strange moves and major exposure make this kind of unnerving for both the leader and the second. –Bryan Burdo FA: Bryan Burdo
	Chain Gang p. 179	★ ★ ★	Far Side	Relief Camp	Exposure is an easily overused word around here, but this baby rocks! –Bryan Burdo FA: Bryan Burdo
	Give Until It Hurts p. 182	★ ★ ★	Far Side	Relief Camp	No pain no gain! –Garth Bruce FA: Bryan Burdo
	A Girl's Best Friend p. 194	★ ★	Far Side	Gritscone	When you care enough to climb the best. –Bryan Burdo FA: Bryan Burdo
	Foreplay p. 184	★ ★	Far Side	Motherland	The nature of the climbing changes dramatically from limestoney to granitic just when the pump is setting in. –Bryan Burdo FA: Bryan Burdo
5.11b	Complete Overhaul p. 179	★ ★	Far Side	Relief Camp	A series of chains link a tricky start, a strenuous mid-wall, and an aesthetic finale on this fine piece of Rhinobilia. –Bryan Burdo FA: Bryan Burdo
	Of Gossamer Shrouds p. 223	★ ★	Far Side	Winter Block	Short, steep traverse. The direct start is currently an open project that's 5.12+. –Leland Windham FA: Leland Windham & Steve Martin 08/01
5.11d	Rough Cut p. 194	★ ★	Far Side	Gritscone	If you enjoy doing back bends in Yoga class then you'lll like this route. –Garth Bruce FA: Bryan Burdo

Difficulty	Route Name	Rating	Area	Wall	Beta
5.12b	Hovering Mother p. 184	★ ★ ★	Far Side	Motherland	Scramble up class 4 to a belay below the monster roof. Take an "embryonic journey" through many body positions (including fetal) as you deliver yourself directly out into the day light and the loving embrace of the chains. –Bryan Burdo FA: Bryan Burdo
	Offspring p. 184	★ ★ ★	Far Side	Motherland	It's a dysfunctional family up here! Somewhat less convoluted, but weird enough to make you wonder. –Bryan Burdo FA: Bryan Burdo
	Flubber p. 184	★	Far Side	Motherland	Wonderful climbing on dirty rock with poor bolt placements. –Bryan Burdo FA: Mike Orr
	Ghost p. 179	★	Far Side	Relief Camp	Reportedly 12b, but my brief acquaintance leaves me to wonder how hard 12b is allowed to be. –Bryan Burdo FA: Keith Wentz
	Green Lantern p. 179	★	Far Side	Relief Camp	Appears to be quite bizarre. –Bryan Burdo FA: Mike Orr

Complete Route Listing

Appendix A

The following tables list all the routes in the Exit 38 area which are Mt Washington, Deception Crags. Check http://www.northbendrock.com for updates.

Difficulty	Rating	Name	Page
5.5	★ ★	Flammable Pajamas	126
	★ ★	So Easy I forgot To Laugh	195
	★ ★	Sumptuous Bits	205
5.6	★ ★ ★ ★	Slumbersome Ridge	79
	★ ★ ★	Homo Erectus	122
	★ ★ ★	In The Middle Again	219
	★ ★ ★	Eating Rocks	217
	★ ★ ★	Eating Dust	217
	★ ★	Lucky Arms	193
	★ ★	Mom There's Pink In My Burger	126
	★ ★	Catatonic	205
	★ ★	Easy Street	154

Difficulty	Rating	Name	Page
5.7	★ ★ ★	Rug Monkey	122
	★ ★ ★	Kiss Of The Crowbar	205
	★ ★ ★	Midnight Scrambler	219
	★ ★ ★	Swerve	219
	★ ★ ★	Swarm	217
	★ ★ ★	Autumnal Equinox	80
	★ ★ ★	Pete's Possum Palace	195
	★ ★	Turf Safari	119
	★ ★	Bottoms Up	126
	★ ★	Party Girl	186
	★ ★	So Funny I Forgot To Rope Up	195
	★ ★	Snaffle Baffler	193
	★ ★	False Pretense	183
	★ ★	Your Sister	154
	★ ★	Needle Magnet	192
	★	Crack One With Me	52
	★	Jiffy Pop	144

Complete Route Listing

Difficulty	Rating	Name	Page
5.8	★ ★ ★ ★	A Castle So Crystal Clear	61
	★ ★ ★	Tunnel Of Love	214
	★ ★ ★	Insomniac	218
	★ ★ ★	Nocturnal Remission	227
	★ ★ ★	A Summer Known As Fall	58
	★ ★ ★	Ultra-Mega Crack	81
	★ ★ ★	Lush	42
	★ ★ ★	Glob Job	122
	★ ★ ★	Glom Don	122
	★ ★ ★	Peanut Brittle	61
	★ ★	Through The Darkness Of Future's Past	63
	★ ★	Chainsaw Chalupa	50
	★ ★	Corner's Inquest	184
	★ ★	Winter Rushing In	205

Difficulty	Rating	Name	Page
5.8	★ ★	On The Outskirts	184
	★ ★	Just Because You're Paranoid Doesn't Mean They're Not After You	42
	★ ★	Chain Gain	182
	★ ★	The Owl	59
	★ ★	Occam's Razor	160
	★ ★	Cornery Bypass	184
	★	Erectile Dysfunction	160
	★	Salutiferous Exaltation through Fusty Waves of an Autonomous and Exsanguinating Corporeality	59

Complete Route Listing

Difficulty	Rating	Name	Page
5.9	★ ★ ★ ★	Absolutely Nothing	156
	★ ★ ★	Killer Bob	62
	★ ★ ★	Awannaduya	61
	★ ★ ★	And The Sun Will Never Rise Again	154
	★ ★ ★	Luscious	42
	★ ★ ★	99 Grit	195
	★ ★ ★	Nocturnal Remission	218
	★ ★ ★	Hurly-Burly	122
	★ ★ ★	Sodflesh	36
	★ ★ ★	Never Was A Cowgirl	61
	★ ★ ★	Endrun	184
	★ ★ ★	Endrun Direct	186
	★ ★ ★	Ultra-Mega Slab	81
	★ ★ ★	November Glaze	205
	★ ★ ★	Siamese Dream	186
	★ ★ ★	Blockhead	156

Difficulty	Rating	Name	Page
5.9	★ ★ ★	Some Drugs	156
	★ ★	Primordial Blues	122
	★ ★	Knife In The Toaster	126
	★ ★	Magnetic Anomaly	192
	★ ★	Black Caboose	156
	★ ★	Strip Clip	138
	★ ★	Semi-Tough	31
	★	Erectile Dysfunction	160
	★	Nature Boy	186
	★	Sobriety	156

Complete Route Listing

Difficulty	Rating	Name	Page
5.10a	★★★★	Just Desert	143
	★★★★	Iguanarama	34
	★★★★	Stairway to Heavin'	93
	★★★★	Endless Bliss	197
	★★★	Gallivant	58
	★★★	Won't Get Fooled Again	149
	★★★	Ellie's Sweet Kiss	211
	★★★	Lovey-Dovey	120
	★★★	Neverigine	134
	★★★	Rhino Rave	161
	★★★	Trappline	41
	★★★	Rhino Relief	182
	★★★	Chica Rapida	194
	★★	Shelf Serve	182
	★★	Toying With My Affections	184
	★★	Q.D. Pie	36
	★	My X Wife (short and easy)	154

Difficulty	Rating	Name	Page
5.10b	★★★★	I Remember Drooling	36
	★★★	Laceration of the Soul	34
	★★★	One Chance Out Between Two Worlds	62
	★★★	Radioactive Decay	34
	★★★	Missing The Taco	207
	★★★	Carnage Before Bedtime	218
	★★★	Lip Service	214
	★★★	Bicycling To Bellingham	217
	★★★	Sheltered Upbringing	184
	★★★	Texas Chainsaw Cheerleaders	50
	★★	Above The Mantle	87
	★★	You're Only Nice To Me When You're Wet	120
	★★	Subliminal	122
	★★	El Astronato	73
	★★	Toying With My Afflictions (Variation)	184
	★	Bwana Be Your Man	119
	★	Strip Clip (Direct)	138
	★	The Joke	154
	★	Controlled Bleeding	123

Complete Route Listing

Difficulty	Rating	Name	Page
5.10c	★★★★	Tropicana	34
	★★★★	Posthumous Joy and Elation	50
	★★★★	Firing Up Bob	70
	★★★	Mr. Fixit	123
	★★★	Winter Walk Within	224
	★★★	Easily Amused	136
	★★★	Love Bucket	138
	★★★	Scrubbing Neon	36
	★★	Slippery When Wet	119
	★★	Chain Smoken	122
	★★	Ten-ish Ooze	36
	★★	Namby-Pamby	120
	★★	Rock Party Vagabond	95
	★★	Booty Squirrel	194
	★★	Rat Face	144
	★★	Powerless	134
	★	Sport Sickness	162
	★	When Roses Form	79
	★	Side Dish	143

Difficulty	Rating	Name	Page
5.10d	★★★★	Appassionata	66
	★★★★	Andante Favori	66
	★★★	Big Mama	138
	★★★	Satoric Inclination	68
	★★★	POSTINSANGUIFI …	70
	★★★	Constantly Amazed	136
	★★★	The Underture	149
	★★★	You're Only Nice To…	120
	★★★	Displacement	212
	★★★	Arbo-Reality	34
	★★★	You'll Only Get Spanked…	82
	★★★	Jugular Vein	182
	★★	Seismic Mardi Gras	223
	★★	Subversive	122
	★★	Super Squish	199
	★★	Paste Human	34
	★★	Firewalk On Me	36
	★★	What Does Bob Want?	57
	★★	Stretcher Case	184
	★	Enema	36

Complete Route Listing

Difficulty	Rating	Name	Page
5.11a	★ ★ ★ ★	The Overture	149
	★ ★ ★ ★	Primus	34
	★ ★ ★ ★	Aperture Ecstasy In A Nocturne Divine	73
	★ ★ ★	Traverse To The Hole	95
	★ ★ ★	Moreplay	184
	★ ★ ★	Strategic Placement	212
	★ ★ ★	Space Face	212
	★ ★ ★	Steep Street	133
	★ ★ ★	Late For Dinner	143
	★ ★ ★	Hangover Helper	120
	★ ★ ★	Architect Rally	138
	★ ★ ★	Patience On The Edge Of Beauty	88
	★ ★ ★	Cascadian Crack	96
	★ ★ ★	Give Until It Hurts	182
	★ ★	Foreplay	184
	★ ★	Drier Adhesive	34
	★ ★	To Crest In Violent Slumber	98
	★ ★	Salterello Presto	75
	★	Semi-Suite	30

Difficulty	Rating	Name	Page
5.11b	★ ★ ★ ★	Crescendo Of The Sarcophagus Bleeding	66
	★ ★ ★	Green Budda	73
	★ ★ ★	Complete Overhaul	181
	★ ★ ★	Negatherion	134
	★ ★ ★	Imbibing Knowledge From A Mortal Furnace	80
	★ ★ ★	Chain Gang	119
	★ ★ ★	Stemming Out Beyond The Grey	80
	★ ★	Of Gossamer Shrouds	224
	★	Easy Money	128
	★	Freedom Hider	70
5.11c	★ ★ ★ ★	Giant	44
	★ ★ ★ ★	The Validity Of Foreverness Twisted...	80
	★ ★ ★ ★	Ataxicrack	94
	★ ★ ★	Give Your Shelf To Me	66
	★ ★ ★	My Evil Plan	50
	★ ★ ★	100% Beef	43
	★ ★	Canine Patrol	138
	★ ★	Semi-Automatic	30

Complete Route Listing

Difficulty	Rating	Name	Page
5.11d	★★★★	My Sorrow Bleeds With Such Delight	94
	★★★	Rude Road	133
	★★★	Liberty Smack	68
	★★★	Inverted Rain Ascending	73
	★★	Rough Cut	194
	★★	The Magician Longs To See	63
	★★	Corporeal Completion	134
	★	Semian Consciousness	29
5.12a	★★★★	Stihl Fingers	50
	★★★★	Empty Martyr Breeding Room	96
	★★★★	Passage	86
	★★★	Mr. Big	44
	★★★	Culture Shock	140
	★★	Under Arrest	133
	★	Stick Boy	119

Difficulty	Rating	Name	Page
5.12b	★★★	Hovering Mother	184
	★★★	Offspring	184
	★★	Bikini Girls With Turbo Drills	43
	★★	Cyanide	44
	★	Flubber	184
	★	Ghost	179
	★	Green Lantern	179
5.12c	★★★	And Empty It Remains	94
	★★★	The Goblet	140
5.12d	★	Positive Vibrations	44
	★	Spartacus	44
5.13a	★	Deliverance	151
5.13b	★★★	Acid Rock	44
	★★★	Crawling From The Wreckage	67
	★	Open Project	151

Best Routes

For those of you who wish you could climb more but can't take more time off work because you owe too much, here are the routes you've got to climb before your job kills you.

Difficulty	Route Name	Area	Wall	Page	Stats	
Best Exit-38 Routes (5.6 – 5.10d)						
5.6	Slumbersome Ridge	Mt Washington	Slumbersome Ridge	98	☐ Lead ☐ Top Rope	☐ Redpoint ☐ Flash
5.7	Kiss Of The Crowbar	Far Side	Interstate Park	207	☐ Lead ☐ Top Rope	☐ Redpoint ☐ Flash
5.8	Ultra-Mega Crack	Mt Washington	Slumbersome Ridge	81	☐ Lead ☐ Top Rope	☐ Redpoint ☐ Flash
5.8	A Castle So Crystal Clear	Mt Washington	Peannacle Point	62	☐ Lead ☐ Top Rope	☐ Redpoint ☐ Flash
5.9	Absolutely Nothing	Deception	We Did Rock	156	☐ Lead ☐ Top Rope	☐ Redpoint ☐ Flash
5.9	Killer Bob	Mt Washington	Peannacle Point	58	☐ Lead ☐ Top Rope	☐ Redpoint ☐ Flash
5.9	Awannaduya	Mt Washington	Peannacle Point	61	☐ Lead ☐ Top Rope	☐ Redpoint ☐ Flash
5.10a	Endless Bliss	Far Side	Gun Show	197	☐ Lead ☐ Top Rope	☐ Redpoint ☐ Flash
5.10a	Iguanarama	Mt Washington	Amazonia	34	☐ Lead ☐ Top Rope	☐ Redpoint ☐ Flash
5.10a	Stairway To Heavin'	Mt Washington	Valley View West	94	☐ Lead ☐ Top Rope	☐ Redpoint ☐ Flash
5.10b	I Remember Drooling	Mt Washington	Amazonia	36	☐ Lead ☐ Top Rope	☐ Redpoint ☐ Flash
5.10c	Tropicana	Mt Washington	Amazonia	34	☐ Lead ☐ Top Rope	☐ Redpoint ☐ Flash
5.10c	Firing Up Bob	Mt Washington	Lost Resort	70	☐ Lead ☐ Top Rope	☐ Redpoint ☐ Flash
5.10d	Appassionata	Mt Washington	Lost Resort	66	☐ Lead ☐ Top Rope	☐ Redpoint ☐ Flash
5.10d	Andante Favori	Mt Washington	Lost Resort	66	☐ Lead ☐ Top Rope	☐ Redpoint ☐ Flash

Best Exit-38 Routes (5.11a – 5.13a)						
Difficulty	**Route Name**	**Area**	**Wall**	**Page**	**Stats**	
5.11a	Primus	Mt Washington	Amazonia	34	☐ Lead ☐ Top Rope	☐ Redpoint ☐ Flash
5.11a	Aperture Ecstasy In A Nocturne Divine	Mt Washington	Alpinia	73	☐ Lead ☐ Top Rope	☐ Redpoint ☐ Flash
5.11b	Crescendo Of The Sarcophagus	Mt Washington	Lost Resort	66	☐ Lead ☐ Top Rope	☐ Redpoint ☐ Flash
5.11c	My Evil Plan	Mt Washington	Chainsaw	52	☐ Lead ☐ Top Rope	☐ Redpoint ☐ Flash
5.11c	The Validity Of Foreverness Twisted	Mt Washington	Slumbersome Ridge	80	☐ Lead ☐ Top Rope	☐ Redpoint ☐ Flash
5.11d	My Sorrow Bleeds With Such Delight	Mt Washington	Valley View West	94	☐ Lead ☐ Top Rope	☐ Redpoint ☐ Flash
5.12a	Mr. Big	Mt Washington	Actual Cave	44	☐ Lead ☐ Top Rope	☐ Redpoint ☐ Flash
5.12a	Passage	Mt Washington	Valley View East	86	☐ Lead ☐ Top Rope	☐ Redpoint ☐ Flash
5.12a	Empty Martyr Breeding Room	Mt Washington	Valley View West	96	☐ Lead ☐ Top Rope	☐ Redpoint ☐ Flash
5.12c	And Empty It Remains	Mt Washington	Valley View West	96	☐ Lead ☐ Top Rope	☐ Redpoint ☐ Flash
5.13a	Acid Rock	Mt Washington	Actual Cave	44	☐ Lead ☐ Top Rope	☐ Redpoint ☐ Flash
5.13a	Crawling From The Wreckage	Mt Washington	Lost Resort	67	☐ Lead ☐ Top Rope	☐ Redpoint ☐ Flash

Linkups

Webster defines linkups as: one or more rock climbing routes that are combined in strange and unusual ways.

1. A short segment that connects two routes that are close to each other.

2. A long segment that connects more than two routes.

3. A ridiculously contrived route that uses a majority of the routes on an entire wall. The ingenious side effect of Grid-Bolting.

Difficulty	Route Name	Rating	Area	Wall	Page	Beta
5.12b	Gob-Smack	★★★	Deception	Nevermind	138	A fine sustained link-up which starts on The Goblet and traverses at the third bolt into "Culture Shock". –Bryan Burdo FA: Leland Windham 10/94
5.10d	Nevermind Traverse	★★★	Deception	Nevermind	134	Strip Clip to Constantly Amused. Can also do a lower traverse from Strip Clip Direct to Rude Road at 5.10c FA: Leland Windham 05/99
5.9	Amazonia Traverse	★★★	Mt Washington	Amazonia	34	Q.D. Pie to Paste Human. FA: Leland Windham 09/96
5.9	Siamese End	★★	Far Side	Slabbabe Patch	186	Midway up Siamese Dream take a left trun onto End Run. FA: Leland Windham 11/96
5.10d	Fire Walk With Me	★★	Mt Washington	Peannacle	63	Start on "Through The Darkness Of Future's Past" and traverse left to "The Magician Longs To See" –Leland Windham FA: Leland Windham 07/97
5.10c	When Roses Form	★★	Mt Washington	Slumbersome Ridge	79	Climb "Crest In Violent Sumber" to overhang then exit right and finsh on "Slumbersome Ridge". FA: Leland Windham 07/98

Additional Area Information

Geology

Most of the rock at Exit 38, fondly called Rhino Stone, is classified by geologists as meta-volcanic. The rock is seriously metamorphosed which translates to very hard and variable formations. These irregular rock features make for some fantastic climbing, including micro sharp edges and overhanging jugs. One thing you won't find is a lot of cracks so it's not the place to show off your big rack.

Facilities

Facilities are limited in each of the climbing areas. Exit 38 has permanent toilets at the Mt Washington parking area but not at the Deception or Far Side parking areas.

Ollalie State Park is ¼ mile past the Deception parking area. The state park has a day time only picnic area, a public telephone, and a permanent toilet by Weeks Falls. (For more information on the Ollalie State Park surf to http://www.parks.wa.gov)

Since North Bend is so close, most out-of-town climbers crash at one of the inexpensive North Bend motels or just surprise a friend in Seattle since it's only a 30 minute drive from North Bend.

Camping

Camping in the Snoqualmie valley is really hit-or-miss. If it's a week day and not close to a holiday then you can probably get find a relatively quite camp spot. If it's a warm and sunny holiday weekend then you'll most likely be spending the night in your car. The camp grounds are normally only open from early May to mid October.

The closest full service privately owned camping area (showers, phone, power, cable tv hookup, etc) to the town of North Bend is Snoqualmie River Camping and RV Park. It's 16.4 miles west of the climbing area just outside the town of Fall City. It's located next to the Snoqualmie River and not one, but the two golf courses next to it. They charge around $20 per night for a tent but for only $8 you can use the facilities (shower, phone, etc) during the day. Note: 25 people per vehicle limit.

The closest State owned camping area (water, toilets, no showers) is Tinkham campground. It is 4 miles further East on Interstate 90 at Exit 42. To reach it take the east bound Exit 42 and turn right at the top of the off ramp and then left onto a dirt road. Follow the dirt road for 1.5 miles and the campground turnoff will be on your left. There is a $7 per day camping fee. It's open from May 16th to Sept 15th.

There are several other campgrounds in the area but personally, I like the Tinkham Campground the best. The camp areas are much larger, it's a short five minute drive from the climbing area, it's next to the South Fork of the Snoqualmie River, and there's usually always an open area. For more information on camping in the area see http://www.parks.wa.gov.

Weather

Exit 38 is usually too cold and wet to climb in the winter months between October and May,but during June, July, and August it's magnificent. Moderate temperature and lots of warm sunny days make it one of the best places to climb in the country.

The Northwest has a weather pattern that is uniquely different from the rest of the United States in that temperatures and rainfall can vary remarkably in a short distance. These differences are due primarily to the varied topography in the region,so even though it may be raining in Seattle,it might be sunny and dry at the climbing areas.

As you can tell from the graph below the monthly temperature (and sunshine) increase steadily in the spring and summer averaging a comfortable 70 degrees Fahrenheit in August.

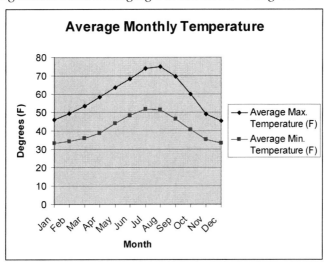

Contrary to popular opinion, the Pacific Northwest does not get more rainfall then the Amazon basin in South America. Actually, Seattle receives less rainfall per year than Atlanta, Miami, or Boston. It will proably rain only if you're in town for the weekend and you're really looking forward to some climbing.

The freezing level in the area is around 2500 feet in the winter. Most of the climbing walls are below 2500 with the exception of the upper walls in the Mt Washington Area at 3000' elevation. By mid-May, most of the snow will have melted away leaving pleasing clean rock.

The graph below shows the average monthly rainfall for the Seattle area in a one year period. As you can see, the climbing areas don't get much traffic in the winter because they're usually covered in wetness but during the summer months the sun does come out, the rain does go away, and the climbing shoes do go on.

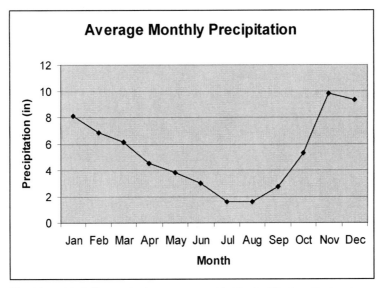

The data points in the graph above were provided by the Western Regional Climate Center. The reporting period is from 1/ 1/1931 to 12/31/2000.

Climbing Area Seasons

The best months to climb at Exit 38 are May through September. Although you can climb there during the winter, given a few days of warm and dry weather, most of the walls are too wet and cold. Here's a quick summary for each of the walls in the areas:

Mt Washington

- Amazonia is the best place to climb in the winter

- The lower walls (Semi, Amazonia, Paradiso, and Actual Cave) usually don't get snow during the winter. The upper walls (Bob's, and Valley View East and West) will get several inches of snow during the winter.

- Club Paradiso is usually wet until late July.

- During the fall, Valley View West is the best place to climb because it receives direct sun throughout the afternoon and early evening.

Deception

- Nevermind Wall stays the driest during the rainy winter.

- Write-Off Rock, Deception Wall, and We Did Rock dry quickly after a shower because of their open exposure to the windy valley, but give them at least 12 hours to dry off before heading up.

- Substation is the wettest during the winter.

Farside

- Most of the walls will be too wet to climb in the winter but, in general, it will be dryer than Mt Washington & Deception.

- The middle section of Overhaul Wall (Motherland), Squishy Bell, and Winter Block receive direct sun and are usually the driest.

- Eastern Block and Gun Show recieve the most sun and warmth during the morning and early afternoon.

Area climbing rules

Most of the routes at Exit 38 are located on public lands and in state parks which are governed by a set of rules. To review the current Washington State Park rules check the informational sheet on the bulletin boards at the climbing areas. The Access Fund Organization also provides a helpful set of climbing rules. Here's a summary from their web site:

The Access Fund is a national, non-profit climbers organization that works to keep climbing areas open and to conserve the climbing environment. Here are some simple guidelines:

•**ASPIRE TO CLIMB WITHOUT LEAVING A TRACE,** especially in environmentally sensitive areas like caves. Chalk can be a significant impact on dark and porous rock—don't use it around historic rock art. Pick up litter, and leave trees and plants intact.

•**DISPOSE OF HUMAN WASTE PROPERLY** Use toilets whenever possible. If toilets are not available, dig a "cat hole" at least six inches deep and 200 feet from any water, trails, campsites, or the base of climbs. *Always pack out toilet paper.* On big wall routes, use a "poop tube" and carry waste up and off with you (the old "bag toss" is now illegal in many areas).

•**USE EXISTING TRAILS** Cutting switchbacks causes erosion. When walking off-trail, tread lightly, especially in the desert where cryptogamic soils (usually a dark crust) take thousands of years to form and are easily damaged. Be aware that "rim ecologies" (the clifftop) are often highly sensitive to disturbance.

• **BE DISCRETE WITH FIXED ANCHORS** *Bolts are controversial and are not a con -venience— don't place them unless they are really necessary.* Camouflage all anchors. Remove unsightly slings from rappel stations (better to use steel chain or welded cold shuts). Bolts sometimes can be used proactively to protect fragile resources—consult with your local land manager.

•**RESPECT THE RULES** and speak up when other climbers don't. Expect restrictions in designated wilderness areas, rock art sites, caves, and to protect wildlife, especially nesting birds of prey. *Power drills are illegal in Wilderness and all national parks.*

•**PARK AND CAMP IN DESIGNATED AREAS** Some climbing areas require a permit for overnight camping.

•**MAINTAIN A LOW PROFILE** Leave the boom box and day-glo clothing at home — the less climbers are heard and seen, the better.

•**RESPECT PRIVATE PROPERTY** Be courteous to land owners. Don't climb where you're not wanted.

•**JOIN THE ACCESS FUND** To become a member, make a tax-deductible donation of $25. For more information surf to www.accessfund.org

Climbing Etiquette

When you reach for that desperate dime-sized hold and come smoking off the wall howling colorful explitives you usually only run the risk of offending other climbers (which is difficult to do). Exit 38 is different. It's not that the local Seattle climbers are overly sensitive, but a large portion of the climbing area has the unique characteristic of being directly on high traffic public trail systems. When you act inappropriate a lot of innocent people and dogs will bear witness to your disrespect and take offense. Be considerate. Your mother may be one of those on the hiking trail.

Acknowledgements

I'd like to thank everyone on the planet for helping me produce this book. There, now that I haven't left anyone out I'd like to further thank Leland Windham and Bryan Burdo for the time and energy they put into technical reviews, route beta, book design, and new climbing routes. In short, this books detail and accuracy, in large part, is due to their involement. If you would like to contact them and express your gratitude for creating some of the best sport routes in the Northwest, or send them donations for their continued route development, surf to http://www.northbendrock.com/contactinfo.

I'd also like to thank Chris Madden and Dave Argento for generously donating their time and expert photography skills, Seattle Mountain Rescue for donating equipment to ensure route safety, my parents (for not using birth control), my neighbors (Beach family) for taking good care of my little one while I was on the more difficult hikes, Dave Wolfe for his meticulous route cleaning, Audra Jensen for her great editing work and Kimberli Morrison for some creative early design ideas, Friends of the Trails for keeping the trailheads clean, Ollalie State and Iron Horse Park rangers for their continual support, all the early book reviewers and local climbers who provided me with valuable feedback and all of the route creators who have unselfishly dedicated their time and effort to creating and maintaining the routes, Doug Gantenbein for lying to me about how easy it is to self publish, Lucky for providing me with details on how to determine if my car contents have been ripped off, and the Department of Natural Resources for supporting the climbing areas. A special thanks to Al Errington who introduced me to the splendor and challenge of the Cascades and has been a wonderful mentor over the years (hence my lack of significant accomplishments).

I'd also like to thank you, the person that purchased the book, for helping me pay off the massive debt I incurred producing this book. I'd also like to say thanks in advance for sending me your comments and corrections to ensure future revisions are complete and accurate.

Area Trivia

This is the part you read when it starts to rain right when you get to the parking area and you believe it's only a brief shower or when you're just sitting in the sun waiting your turn for a route or …

- Best wall name : We Did Rock (put "We Did" in front of each route name)

- Shortest route : Hall Creek Wall, route - "Sport Sickness"

- Longest route: Endless Bliss (16 bolts) in the Far Side area on the Gun Show wall.

- First route created: Giant – 9/1993. Most recent route: Lip Service – 8/2002

- Strangest route name: Salutiferous Exaltation through Fusty Waves of an Autonomous and Exsanguinating Corporeality. Translation – Climb this route or you're going to Windham Hell.

- Alan Watts reportedly took 20 years to write the Smith Rock Climbing Guide. This Book reportedly took 20 months to write.

- The Snolqualmie Falls drops 268 feet, 100 feet further than Niagara.

- In 1890 Charlie Anderson made the first unsuccessful parachute jump into the canyon of Snoqualmie Falls.

- In 1892 North Bend consisted of a small wooden hotel, a small saloon, and one general store. It's gone down hill ever since.

- The first year Snoqualmie Pass was open through the winter was 1931-32.

- In 1882 North Bend (and the surrounding area) was the world's largest producer of Hops. Most were sold to Germany and England.

- The City of North Bend was originally named "Snoqualmie", then "Mountain View", and finally in 1906 "North Bend".

- The Iron Horse trail extends from North Bend to the Iowa border.

- The main Far Side trail is also affectionately know as "Bird House" trail because of the mysterious bird houses which adorn the trail all the way to the ridge crest.

- The Exit 38 road was actually part of the old two lane Interstate 90 highway. The old two lane Interstate 90 highway was part of the the original wagon trail.

Non Sequitur Quotes

1. The Big Stick Clip (Boner Draw). For those routes you would like to climb but don't have the skill. –Leland Windham

2. Do they make coffee cup holders for climbing harnesses? –Dee Boka

3. I think if I stopped eating so much raw cabbage possums would stop trying to sleep with me. –Bryan Burdo

4. RAD-administered, trailhead mammograms are the future. –Al Errington

5. When are you going to publish this damn climbing book? –Leland Windham

6. Sweet. –Gary Perkowski

7. You #!@! Bastard (after seeing my new Nikon D100 camera). –Chris Madden

8. Oh yeah, I got ya. –Leland Windham

9. We'll play just one more game of AOE and then we'll get some sleep. –Jason Suess

10. No, really, officer, this is a friend's truck and I'm sure it's licensed. –Sarah Leonard

11. Where can I get keys to the fire training access road gate? –Bryan Burdo

12. …and if you poke them with a stick they play dead and then you can… -Tim O'Brien

13. Tell me again why everything has to be three stars on Interstate Park? –Bryan Burdo

14. Everyone should have a wire brush on their harness so they can clean the route after they climb it. –Dave Wolfe

15. Get'em in Son, Get'em In! –Eric Andrae

16. My heel still hurts from that damn boob belay! –Kurt Griffis

17. 5.11a? I don't think so - 5.10b at most… -Mellisa Haltuch

18. Sleep is a waste of time. –Rich Brown

19. Daddy, can we go? -Ellie Bruce

About The Books Creation

It all started when I was blessed with a little girl I could call my own back in the summer of 1999. She wasn't part of my plan at the time but lucky thing it happened because, as every parent will tell you, it changed everything in my life, and I mean everything.

Author Garth Bruce
(Photo by Ellie Bruce)

Prior to my little one, I had been working in, what was then, the lucrative computer industry since my graduation from college and doing my best to be self serving and self centered. My beautiful little girl comes into this world, and I decide to take a few years off to raise her. I knew work would always be there, but she wouldn't be, so I figured why not? It was fun to let the brain regress to the level of an infant but after 4 months, I started to get scared because I was losing contact with the world. It was good to let my heart beat to another rhythm, but I quickly realized I was giving too much of myself to her thus losing part of who I was. I'm sure a lot of you climbers who don't have kids can relate if you remember what it's like climbing a significant wall. You really become the wall because you have too. All your instincts center your attention, sharpen your focus. But, you can't stay on the wall too long or your friend Mr. Brain starts to overload from too much of a good thing.

During the fall of 1999 I decided to take a few digital pictures of my favorite climbing routes at Exit 32 and Exit 38 to post on my web site. This was something that I could easily do with my little girl. Just put a couple of diapers on her, stuff her in the backpack with something interested tied to the back of my hat and enjoy the day. What I quickly realized was that I had taken a picture of virtually every wall in the Exit 38 area! At that point I thought why not just add all the routes? Using a laptop computer and the digital camera it only took me a few hours per wall and by the end of the summer I had most of the area digitized. I put it all together during the winter of 2000 and posted it in the spring of 2001 at www.deceptioncrags.com.

I thought that was it, but a lot of people kept asked me "When are you and Bryan (Burdo) publishing the new book?" Well, I hadn't talked to Bryan about a book, but I thought, why not give him the digital pictures if he was doing a book? To make a long story short I started working on the book during the fall of 2001. One year later I self published the book and created the NorthBendRock.com web site.

The book design was born primarily from advances in digital photography technology. The digital camera (Nikon 990) allowed me to take multiple pictures of a wall, quickly download them onto my laptop, and stitch them together into one complete picture. For the most part it works but there is the problem of lens and image distortion.

To capture the entire wall, I had to use wide angle lenses. (Remember, this is the Northwest where if you're 10 feet off a trail you run the risk of getting hopelessly lost in a jungle of vegetation.) A wide angle lens distorts the images because of its convex curvature, referred to as linear distortion. What this means in English is when you look at the wall/routes pictures you will notice a slight distortion at the edges (that's the lens) and you will also notice that the edges of some pictures are irregular (that's the software). Although the picture distortion can be annoying, I felt it's much better than just a topo drawing.

I used Microsoft Word for the document layout and Microsoft Photodraw for the route overlays on the wall pictures and the 3D map text overlays. The software application MGI Photo Vista was used to stitch the images together if more than one picture was needed to capture the entire wall. I also used MGI Photo Vista to create the panoramic images on the web site. The 3D maps were created using the software Terrain Navigator from the company MapTech. Terrain Navigator was also used to generate the the elevation profiles from data points collected from my Garmin III GPS.

Most of the climbing photos were taken using my Nikon D100 digital camera. Chris Madden and David Argento also took a lot of great photos using a Nikon F100 SLR camera. To capture the wall and route images, I used a Nikon 990 digital camera with a Nikon wide angle lense.

Rock climbing is a sport that the young and spry, and old and wise can enjoy. The old "it's too dangerous", or "are you nuts?" stereotypes are gone and today people of all types and ages drive the short distances to enjoy a safe and enriching sport. By basing this book on photos and keeping it simple I hope people of all types and ages will be more inclined to try this safe and enriching sport.

I feel very fortunate to have been able to the take the last few years to develop the web site and book. I've made a lot of new friends and learned several valuable lessons during the course of the project. I'm not sure what I'll be doing next. I could throw myself back into the world of silicon but with any luck my computer skills are now obsolete. More likely I'll have my little girl, back tied to a rock or tree, belaying me up "just one more" irresistible route.